FAMILY TELEVISION:

CULTURAL POWER AND DOMESTIC LEISURE

by David Morley

A Comedia book
published by Routledge
London and New York

First published 1986 by Comedia Publishing Group
Reprinted 1988, 1993, 1999

Transferred to Digital Printing 2005

by Routledge
2 Park Square, Milton Park, Abingdon, Oxon, OX14 4RN

Simultaneously published in the USA and Canada
by Routledge
270 Madison Ave, New York NY 10016

Routledge is an imprint of the Taylor & Francis Group

British Library Cataloguing in Publication Data
A catalogue record for this book is available from the British Library

Library of Congress Cataloging in Publication Data
A catalog record for this book is available from the Library of Congress

ISBN 0-415-03970-3

Acknowledgements

I would like to acknowledge the help and support given to me by a number of people, without whom this book would not have been written – although that does not mean that any of them are to blame for the inadequacies of the final product. First, I must thank the IBA, and Bob Towler in particular, for funding my research when no other agency was prepared to do so. I must also thank Philip Corrigan, with whom a number of the initial ideas were formulated; Richard Paterson, Valerie Walkerdine and Charlotte Brunsdon, all of whom offered valuable comments and criticisms of earlier drafts; and Stuart Hall, whose encouragement has always been invaluable. I must also thank everyone at Comedia for their support during the very long period of gestation of this book, but especially Sue Field Reid, who has retyped it so often that she could probably recite large chunks of it in her sleep. Finally, my thanks must also go to the families who co-operated with me in the research.

Contents

Introduction   7

Foreword   11

1. Understanding the uses of television   13

2. Television in the family   18

3. Research development: from 'decoding' to viewing
    context   40

4. Objectives, methodology and sample design   50

5. Family interviews   56

    (i)   Unemployed families   56

    (ii)   C2 families   87

    (iii) C1 families   112

    (iv)   B families   126

6. Television and gender   146

    Afterword   174

    Notes   176

Introduction

In spite of its modest claims, this is in fact a seminal piece of research into the question of the social uses of television. It delivers new insights and genuinely provides what many other studies misleadingly label as "findings". More significantly, it makes us look again at what we thought was obvious, thereby opening up new questions. Like all good research, it does not appear out of the blue but is part of an unfolding project of work on which David Morley has been engaged for over a decade. Those not already familiar with its earlier stages will want to set this latest instalment in the context of the study of *Nationwide*, with Charlotte Brunsdon (BFI Monograph, 1978: Brunsdon and Morley), Morley's own follow-up, *The Nationwide Audience* (also a BFI Monograph, 1980) and the article in *Culture, Media, Language* (1980) entitled "Texts, Readers, Subjects", which critically reflected on the evolving theoretical line of argument.

This body of work helped to bring about the long-overdue demise of old-style audience surveys, with their monolithic conception of "the viewer" and simple-minded notion of message, meaning and influence, which for so long dominated media studies. It helped to inaugurate a new set of interests in a more active conception of the audience and of the codes and competences involved in establishing variant readings. This approach was differentiated from other work on "texts" (from which it nevertheless learned a good deal) by its persistent attention to the social dimensions of viewing and interpretation, alongside the textual aspects.

Despite this suggestive line of inquiry, Morley has had to hustle around to persuade anyone that the project was worth funding, and the whole line of inquiry has thus been subject to unnecessary and damaging fits and starts – an episode which does little credit to those organisations which currently dispose of research funding in the field. The fact that the pilot research for this monograph was completed at all is due to the support of Bob Towler, director of research at the IBA, to whom credit is due; and, of course, to Comedia, which Morley helped to found and which, far from being simply the publisher of the report, is itself part of the whole project in a larger sense.

Morley has now considerably extended the range of research traditions on which he is drawing. This current piece of research shows the influence, *inter alia*, of recent work on texts, readers and discourse, further work on the encoding–decoding model, feminist work on romance, family studies – as well as more "mainstream" work on leisure activities, time budgets and the factors which influence viewer commitment, choice and "switching".

The central idea behind this piece of work was simply to explore further "the increasingly varied uses to which the television set can now be put". Television viewing has to be seen less and less as an isolated and individual, more and more as a social, even a collective, activity. Typically, it takes place in families (or whatever intimate social group now substitutes for them). However, we know next to nothing about how this everyday domestic context influences what we view, how we view, or what sense we make of it. We know almost as little about what role television plays in family relationships – how family interactions influence the choices we make about viewing or the uses to which we put what we view. We know even less, if this is possible, about how we actually behave (as opposed to how we would like to think we behave) when the set is on – either our conduct towards the screen or towards each other.

David Morley has tried to find out by interviewing in depth a sample of families from different social backgrounds. Suspecting, quite rightly, that the standard techniques – fixed-choice questionnaire, sample survey and self-recorded diary – would tell us more about what producers and advertisers wanted to hear than what was actually going on, he has gone instead for the extended, unstructured interview and a qualitative methodology. The monograph reports, in a clear but necessarily tentative way, what he discovered, setting it succinctly in the context of related research (much of it new to critical researchers, who are sometimes too impatient of "mainstream" work) and giving us the benefit of extensive verbatim quotes from the interviewees so that we can see for ourselves how they framed, in their own words, the viewing experience.

Television viewing, the choices which shape it and the many social uses to which we put it, now turn out to be irrevocably active and social processes. People don't passively absorb subliminal "inputs" from the screen. They discursively "make sense" of or produce "readings" of what they see. Moreover, the "sense" they make is related to a pattern of choices about what and when to view which is constructed within a set of relationships constituted by the domestic and familial settings in which it is taking place. The "rational consumer in a free and perfect market", so beloved of advertisers, audience research departments and rational-choice economists alike, is a myth. The activity has to be understood, analysed and explained in terms of the everyday domestic settings in which it characteristically occurs. In this way, Morley very suggestively brings together two lines of critical inquiry which have tended to be kept in strict isolation – "questions of interpretation and questions of use". Viewing, he insists, has to be seen as a constitutive part of the "familial or domestic relations through which we construct our lives". This point is reinforced by the variety of uses other than "viewing" to which we put the set – and the variety of other activities we seem perfectly capable of sustaining while we view. Viewing is almost always accompanied by argument, comment, debate and discussion. Programmes are surrounded, if not totally submerged, by an incessant flow of other activity and talk, only some of it television-related. The "talk" about television is both critical – it is comment on and about something we do not in any simple way "confuse" with reality – and at the same time sustains involvement and identification (in varying degrees of intensity) with what is on the screen, as well as maintaining interactions with other people. These different dimensions and modes of viewing – contrary to received psychological wisdom – are not mutually incompatible. Moreover, the comment, far from destroying pleasurable identification, seems to be actually part of the pleasure: we enjoy the way the televisual flow is incorporated into the "flows" of everyday domestic life. This should oblige us to rethink many of our common-sense ideas about the so-called confusions between "reality" and "fantasy" in television. People seem to be perfectly well aware of the fact that *EastEnders* is not "real life". However, this does not seem in any way to diminish their capacity for involvement in the fabricated worlds of fictional television. Our actual modes of relating to television are far more complex than the protocols of most research suppose.

So are the "uses" we normally make of the medium. Even in this pilot research Morley is able to demonstrate how various are the activities which accompany television viewing and how varied are the social uses to which it is put. Viewing can be used to provide the occasion for family interaction, or to "create space", even when the living-room is crammed with other people. It can forge solidarities, establish alliances between family members or just provide a much-needed excuse for cuddling up. The medium thus has become integrated into the everyday processes and codes of family interaction. Around it a complex web of customary procedures and rituals, rules and principles develop. It is enveloped by the tensions of negotiations which accompany any form of decision-making in families. Choices about what and when to view, and control of the switch, are – like everything else – allocated along the lines of power and relationship which intersect all families ("havens in a heartless world, indeed"). As we might have predicted, gender turns out to be one of the main principles which structure and shape this field.

Throughout all this, Morley makes subtle use of the notions of variability, diversity and difference. We are not "viewers" with a single identity, a monolithic set of preferences and repetitive habits of viewing, all exposed to a single channel and type of "influence" and therefore behaving in predictably uniform ways. We are all, in our heads, several different audiences at once, and can be constituted as such by different programmes. We have the capacity to deploy different levels and modes of attention, to mobilise different competences in our viewing. At different times of the day, for different family members, different patterns of viewing have different "saliences". Here the monolithic conceptions of the viewer, the audience or of television itself have been displaced – one hopes forever – before the new emphasis on difference and variation. It is these variant mappings between these different factors in the social contexts of viewing which Morley has begun to trace. What the mappings reveal, in sum, is the fine-grained interrelationships between meaning, pleasure, use and choice.

The study offers many other rich and illuminating insights which will reward the reader who is prepared to read and work with the text. It is sufficiently open-ended, displaying the basis of its own evidence and inferences, to withstand contrary interpretation and positively to invite criticism and further development. In this exceedingly complicated territory, these qualities are the only guarantees we have of honest, original and scientific work. Who, in the well-heeled world of research "centres of excellence", is currently offering more?

1986   *Stuart Hall*

Foreword

This book is based on a pilot research project funded by the Independent Broadcasting Authority, which was conducted in the spring of 1985, investigating television viewing in a small number of families from different social backgrounds. Because of the small size of the sample (and the restricted definition of household type employed in its construction) care must be taken in attempting to generalise from my findings. The research was of a preliminary nature, and uses qualitative techniques, aiming to pursue issues about programme preference and viewing behaviour in depth, so as to raise questions which could usefully be pursued at a later stage, both in extended qualitative work with a broader sample and in survey work.

In particular it must be borne in mind that this research was based on a sample of respondents who were quite deliberately selected as belonging to one specific type of household – the traditional nuclear family, with both parents living together with their dependent children. Moreover, all the families were white, and all lived in one area of inner London. All research samples must have their limits and these were the particular limits which I adopted. I am well aware that matters may well be quite different in households of other types (and the nuclear family is now in a distinct minority) and among families from different ethnic and geographical backgrounds. Furthermore, while my sample was intended to include a mix of families from different class backgrounds, in practice the sample is dominated by families from a working-class or lower middle-class background. Thus the findings presented below can only be claimed to be representative, at most, of viewing patterns within one type of household, drawn from one particular ethnic and geographic context and from a relatively narrow range of class positions.

1

Understanding the uses of television

Centrally, this project was designed to investigate two different types of questions, concerning, on the one hand, how television is used within different families and, on the other hand, how television material is interpreted by its audience. Questions of interpretation and questions of use have not previously been investigated in relation to each other. In the past they have been the exclusive provinces of different research traditions – the one within the realms of literary/semiological perspectives, the other within the field of sociological "leisure studies". My project was designed to overcome this unproductive form of segregation, in the belief that only a more holistic research perspective – which takes account of *both* kinds of issues – could successfully pursue these urgent questions about the television audience.

My central thesis was that the changing patterns of television viewing could only be understood in the overall context of family leisure activity. Previous work in this area has tended to focus too narrowly on one or another side of a pair of interlinked issues which need, in fact, to be considered together: these are the issues of how viewers make sense of the materials they view, and the social (and primarily familial) relations within which viewing is conducted.

One tradition of work (in film cultural studies) has concentrated on the semiology of the text/image and the problem of textual meaning, only latterly registering the problematic status of the "reader" to whom the text/image is addressed, and that largely in isolation from the social context of viewing. On the other side, the sociological/leisure studies perspective has concentrated (as has much of the broadcasting organisations' own research) on counting patterns of viewing behaviour with scant regard for how meanings (and thus choices) get made in this process.

My premise here was that the respective strengths of these two different perspectives needed to be combined, so as to consider problems of audience decoding/choice in the context of family leisure. Too often, the fact that television is predominantly a *domestic medium* and that viewing is largely done "in" the family is either ignored, or is "registered" only to be assumed away as a pre-given "backdrop" to the activity, rather than being directly investigated.

Television viewing may be a "privatised" form of activity, by comparison with cinema-going for example, but it is still largely conducted within, rather than outside of, social relations – in this case the social relations of the family or household.

My own increasing interest in the analysis of the domestic viewing context can best be understood in relation to my previous involvement in the *Nationwide* research project at the Centre for Contemporary Cultural studies in Birmingham.[1] Originally it had been hoped to follow up the investigation of differential patterns of "decoding" of *Nationwide* in that project with supplementary interviews with respondents at home. In the end, because of the practical limitations of time, funding, etc., that dimension was never pursued and the *Nationwide* project stopped short at the analysis of the pattern of differential "decodings" offered by groups of respondents when interviewed in groups (primarily in the context of educational instructions).

While I would, of course, argue that the findings in that project remain of considerable interest, I had subsequently come to feel that it was vital to pursue finally the question of how people watched television in its more "natural" setting, at home with their families. In short, my focus of interest has thus shifted from the analysis of the pattern of differential audience "readings" of particular programme materials, to the analysis of the domestic viewing context itself – as the framework within which "readings" of programmes are (ordinarily) made.

This research project was also designed to investigate the increasingly varied uses to which the television set can now be put. We are now in a situation where people can "do" a number of things with their television set besides watching broadcast television. This question goes beyond the implications of the increasing range of options in broadcast television (Channel Four, breakfast television) and beyond the implications of cable and satellite television in providing yet further choices.

We now confront a situation where the television set, while remaining the "family hearth", can be used to videotape broadcast television and watch this at a later time; to watch rented and bought videotape material; to call up "electronic pages" of information (Teletext, Prestel, Oracle); and as a space on which either to play interactive video games or to display computerised data and to make calculations.

Audience research needs to explore the implications of this set of changes if we are to understand the changing significance of the "box in the corner", in the context of the growing impact of new technology, both in diversifying the nature of the home-based leisure opportunities and in re-emphasising the existence of the home as the principal site of leisure.

A further premise of the analytical framework of the research project is that the social dimensions of "watching television" – the social relations within which viewing is performed as an activity – have to be brought more directly into focus if we are properly to understand television audiences' choices of, and responses to, their viewing.

Here I have attempted to build upon some of the insights of the "uses and gratifications" approach to audience research – asking what people do with the media – but taking the dynamic *unit* of consumption to be more properly the family/household rather than the individual viewer. This is to raise questions about how the television set is handled in the home, how decisions are made – by which family members, at what times, as to "what to watch" – and how responses to different kinds of material are discussed within the family, etc. In short, this represents an attempt to analyse individual viewing activity within the social (and primarily household/familial) relations in which it commonly operates. Audience research which ignores the social/familial position of the viewer cannot comprehend a number of key determinations relating to both viewing "choices" and responses. These involve questions of differential power, responsibility and control within the family, at different times of the day or evening.

The further premise is that the use of the television set has to be understood in the wider context of the other, competing and complementary, leisure activities (hobbies, interests, pastimes, etc.) in which viewers are engaged. Television clearly is a primary leisure activity, but previous research has tended merely to investigate leisure options as a range of separate and unrelated activities to be listed, rather than to investigate the relations between "watching television" and other leisure activities. This project was designed to investigate the relations in which television viewing can be seen to structure – and be structured – by other leisure activities, in different ways for viewers in different social/familial positions.

"Watching television" cannot be assumed to be a one-dimensional activity which has equivalent meaning or significance at all times for all who perform it. I was concerned to identify and investigate the differences hidden behind the catch-all description "watching television"; both the differences between the choices made by different kinds of viewers in relation to different viewing options, and the differences (of attention and comprehension) between different viewers' responses to the same viewing materials – differences which are masked by the finding that they all "watched" a given programme.

I was concerned to explore both differences within families, between their different members, and differences between families in different social and cultural contexts. I would argue that it is only in this context – that of the wider fields of social and cultural determinations which frame the practices of viewing – that individual "choices" and "responses" can be understood.

My argument is that the viewing patterns for broadcast television can only be comprehended in the context of this wider set of questions concerning life-style, work situation, and *their* interrelation with the scheduling limitations of broadcast television. "Availability" is thus a dynamic concept which relates "which groups can (or wish to) watch, when (and with how much attention)?" *and* "what types of programme are being broadcast and at what times?" – plus the availability of certain *types* of televisual material from off-air or hired/purchased video recordings.

As Mallory Wober has argued,[2] most television "research" is in fact *measurement*, i.e., quantitative registration of how many people of what kinds are watching particular programmes *and* to what degree particular samples of people thought certain programmes interesting and/or enjoyable. The results, as he argues, offer bases for research, but are not research in and of themselves.

Moreover, the ways in which the information is gathered for these surveys ignore the contexts of use of television. By asking individuals to complete diaries (for the audience appreciation measurements) of which programmes they watched, reasons for such choices are not discovered. Moreover, the placing of the television set in a context of differential users (and differential uses) is never raised. Measuring does not address issues like this. Even that minority of audience research which is concerned with *evaluation* as opposed to measurement, is insufficiently comparative. By "comparative" I am referring to four types of comparisons:

(a) Comparisons as between channels
(b) Comparisons as between different types of programme
(c) Comparisons as between different groups of viewers
(d) Comparisons as between different uses of the television set (in terms of different types of televisual material and different groups of viewers).

This research programme was designed, then, to pursue a number of related concerns:

(i) the need for a fuller and more flexible understanding of (rather than simply measuring) viewers' reactions to material transmitted. One important question here is that of developing differential "appreciation-indexes" in relation to the life-styles and cultural backgrounds of different categories of viewers.

(ii) the need for an understanding of the *grounds* of such individual choices and reactions, which takes account of the ways in which individual choices and viewer reactions are situated in and affected by particular social and cultural contexts.

I was also concerned to generate a comparative study of specific social groups in relation to channel-choice and programme-type commitment:

Choice: the significance of *scheduling* in relation to (a) television use, (b) channel switching and channel loyalty, and (c) life-patterns of different social groups, and different members of families within the same social group.

Commitment: the significance of the internal characteristics and structure of different *types of programmes* within television use in relation to different social groups and different members of families within the same social group.

The objectives were:

(1) to complement existing measurement data;
(2) to deepen our understanding of what patterns of viewing relate to which social groups;
(3) to reconceptualise notions of "appreciation" in relation to types of programme.

In particular, this project was designed to explore in detail, with a deliberately limited universe, the factors which frame "viewing behaviour". The focus was on the "how" and "why" questions which lie unexplained behind the patterns of viewing behaviour revealed by large-scale survey work (as discussed, for instance, in Goodhart *et al.*). My objective was to produce a fuller understanding of the questions (for example, the grounds for and differential criteria employed in particular viewing choices) which need to be understood in order to pave the way for more productive large-scale survey work across a larger sample.

In short, by investigating how factors such as programme type, family position and cultural background interrelate to produce the dynamics of family viewing behaviour and responses, I aimed to produce a more developed conceptual model of viewing behaviour in the context of family leisure which would then be available for testing across a wider sample.

Television in the family

Despite frequent moral panics about "television and the family" we still know very little about how families as distinct from individuals (who, after all, mostly live in families or households of some kind) interact with and use television in their everyday lives. The perspective employed in this project has been one which attempts to redress this imbalance and to consider television viewing as a social activity, one which is conducted within the context of the family as a set of social relations, rather than as a merely individual activity, or as the activities of a collection of individuals who merely happen to live in the same household. The need for this approach is surely now beyond argument. As the introduction to *Communication Research Trends*' issue on "TV and Family Communication" put it:

> "As long ago as 1972 the US Surgeon General's Advisory Committee Report on TV and Social Behaviour requested that TV be studied in the home environment. Ten years later, the update of the Surgeon General's report 'Television and Behaviour' called once again for more studies on family interaction with TV and for a research approach which uses the family or peer group as the unit of analysis."[1]

This perspective has a number of implications. First, let us return to the comments above on the disjuncture between my findings in this project and the generally accepted thesis that people are just as likely to view types of programme which they claim not to like as they are to view their claimed programme preference. James Webster and Jacob Wakshlag go some considerable way towards explaining why stated preferences fail to match up with observed viewing behaviour by the simple expedient of taking into account the influence of "others" (other members of the family or household) on programme choice – that is, "the role that group viewing plays in mediating the free exercise of individual preference".[2] As they explain, many theorists have assumed that television programme choice is a direct result of individual programme preference, and that, as a consequence, patterns of stated programme preference should be manifest in viewing behaviour. As they note, Goodhart *et al.* concluded that in terms of recorded viewing behaviour "there is no special tendency across the population for people who watch one programme of a given type also to watch others of the same type".[3] This conclusion has led many to believe that statements of programme type preference, given that they are poor predictors of viewing behaviour, are of little interest or significance.

In fact, as Webster and Wakshlag show, when respondents view alone, their programme choice is more consistent with reference to programme type (as indeed it is when they view consistently with the same group of other people). A large part of the "gap" between individuals' stated programme preferences and their actual viewing behaviour is to be accounted for by the effects of others, and the need to accommodate and negotiate with their preferences as to what is to be viewed. In short, a lot of people's viewing is not of their own choosing. As they put it, contrary to their original hypothesis that an increased incidence of group viewing would result in a reduction of programme type loyalty:

> "Group viewing *per se* did not reduce programme type loyalty. Rather, it appeared that when a composition of the viewing unit varied across time [for example, when a respondent viewed with varying combinations of family members], programme type loyalty declined. When the viewing unit was constant, as was the case with a solitary viewer or an unchanging group, programme type loyalty was heightened."[4]

We are, in short, discussing television viewing in the context of domestic life, which as we all know is a somewhat complex matter. To expect that we could treat the individual viewer making programme choices as if he or she were the rational consumer in a free and perfect market is surely the height of absurdity when we are talking of people who live in families (unless my own experience of families is, for some reason, unrepresentative). After all, for most people, viewing takes place within the context of what Sean Cubitt has called "the politics of the living room" where, as he puts it, "if the camera pulls us in, the family pulls us out", and where the people you live with are likely to disrupt, if not shatter, your communication with the "box in the corner".[5]

Let us consider the problem from another angle. Herman Bausinger's research provides the following account of what "switching on the television" can mean – and it clearly doesn't necessarily mean that one wants to watch the television: "Early in the evening we watch very little TV. Only when my husband is in a real rage. He comes home, hardly says anything and switches on the

TV."[6] As Bausinger notes, in this case "pushing the button doesn't signify 'I would like to watch this', but rather 'I would like to see and hear nothing' or 'I don't want to talk to anybody'." Conversely, he notes, later the opposite case where "the father goes to his room, while the mother sits down next to her eldest son and watches the sports review with him. It does not interest her, but it is an attempt at making contact."[7]

By way of a protocol, Bausinger also helpfully provides us with a number of points to bear in mind in relation to domestic media consumption:

"1)   To make a meaningful study of the use of the media, it is necessary to take different media into consideration, the media ensemble which everyone deals with today... The recipient integrates the content of different media...

2)   As a rule the media are not used completely, nor with full concentration... the degree of attention depends on the time of the day, or moods, the media message competes with other messages...

3)   The media are an integral part of the way the everyday is conducted [for example, the newspaper as a necessary constituent part of 'breakfast'] and [media] decisions are constantly crossed through and influenced by non-media conditions and decisions.

4)   It is not a question of an isolated, individual process, but of a collective process. Even when reading a newspaper one is not truly alone, it takes place in the context of the family, friends, colleagues...

5)   Media communication cannot be separated from direct personal communication. Media contacts are materials for conversation."[8]

This last point is also germane to the hoary old question as to whether television is killing (or indeed, has already killed) the "art of conversation". Simon Hoggart, writing in *New Society*, put the point well:

"What TV does furnish is a shared experience which actually increases the amount of conversation. In factories and offices across the land people earnestly debate what they saw on the screen last night [compare this with my own family interviews] where once they might have discussed the sales manager's love life, the weather, or the shortcomings of the head of faculty."[9]

In fact, the whole basis of the predominant cultural snobbery which sees almost any activity as superior to "watching television" (and which confers prestige on "not watching television" almost as an activity in itself) lies in the assumption that television is capable, somehow, of obliterating the processes of domestic communication that would otherwise occur in the home. As my findings indicate, this is far too simple a picture of a process in which (as Bausinger shows) media and domestic communications exist in all manner of symbiotic intertwinings.

Even those who would argue that television has somehow "harmed" domestic conversations are sometimes forced to admit that television itself has also made significant contributions to the "art of conversation". Here is Nancy Banks-Smith, writing in the *Guardian* about the contribution of situation comedies to the development of the art:

> "Television has not exactly killed conversation; it has eaten it alive, woofing it down wholesale as a cat might a canary. 'Where has it gone?' thinks the bereaved owner, looking wildly round the living-room. 'It was here a moment ago, chirruping away.' And then the television set starts to sing.
>
> The best conversation heard around most homes in the last twenty years has been in situation comedies. People with nothing better to do talk best. Hancock alone on a Saturday night, Dud and Pete in a wardrobe discussing the womb, Foggy, Clegg and Compo in their second childhood, Fletcher in prison. Conversation actually seems to improve in captivity."[10]

As Thomas Lindlof and Paul Traudt argue,[11] many media scholars have tended to view television viewing as somehow "supplanting family functions", rather than investigating how media resources are adapted to families' economic and cultural (or psychological) needs. This can involve quite elementary considerations – such as, for instance, the use of television to create personal space in a restricted physical environment. As Lindlof and Traudt note,[12] "in higher, density families... TV viewing may function as a way of avoiding conflicts or lessening tensions in lieu of spatial privacy." These authors also make most convincingly a very basic point about the problems with a lot of media research to date. They note that much research has concentrated on "questions of *why*, to the exclusion of *what* and *how*. [Scholars] have attempted to describe causes and consequences of televiewing without an adequate understanding of what it is and how it gets done". They rightly argue that in order for "many of the central theoretical and policy questions to be satisfactorily framed, let alone answered, a number of prerequisite questions concerning *what the act of TV viewing entails* [my emphasis – D.M.] for all family members, need to be posed and investigated".[13]

The dominant image of the relationship between the family and television (or the media in general) is one in which the media are seen as having a primarily disruptive effect on household routines and family relationships. In this picture the media's influence is seen as primarily negative and disruptive. However, it is perfectly possible to pose this issue the other way round. Rather than simply thinking of television having a disruptive effect on the household, one can examine the ways in which television provides family members with different schedules for gathering, the ways in which television provides acceptable zones for private pursuits, the ways in which television programming does not so much intrude on existing family activities as provide organising centres or focuses for new types of communicative contexts. As Lindlof and Traudt put it, "Family members eat and drink with their television viewing, engage in content-related and content-unrelated talk, iron clothes, study, dress, undress, daydream and so on." James Lull has also provided us with a more useful way of thinking about the relationship between television and the family. He provides a model of this relationship in which television can be seen "to play a central role in the methods which family members and other social units employ purposefully to interact normatively within their own special everyday realities".[14]

The point here is that, considered in this way, television can be seen to provide in one sense an alibi, in another sense a context, for encounters between family members, where the content of the television programme they are watching together may often simply serve as a common experiental ground for conversation. In this kind of instance, television is being used for something which is more than entertainment. It is being used as a focus, as a method for engaging in social interaction with others. So, far from simply disrupting family interaction, television is being used purposefully by family members to construct the occasions of their interactions, and to construct the context within which they can interact. It is being used to provide the reference points, the ground, the material, the stuff of conversation.

Family studies

In this connection it is especially interesting that some of the best recent work on television and the family has been generated not within the orbit of media studies but within the orbit of psychology and family studies. Thus, Irene Goodman writing in the *Journal of Family Issues*[15] provides a very interesting perspective. As she puts it, the primary focus of much work in the past has been on the effects of television viewing on behaviour. By contrast, she argues that what is important in examining the role of television in family life is not simply the matter of studying effects on family members. It also involves looking at television as a phenomenon that serves a whole range of social purposes, the study of which can shed light on general family functioning. As she puts it:

> "The working assumption [of] traditional research dealing with the effects of television is that television is a medium of information, entertainment, education, and/or an indirect informative agent in the area of values and behaviour. However, if it is assumed that television not only is used by family members for these traditional reasons but also has other functions (for example, as a companion, scapegoat, mediator, boundary marker between family members, to schedule their other activities, as a reward or punishment, as a bartering agent, and so on) then a new set of research opportunities present themselves. By studying the role that TV plays in the realisation of these other purposes, we are in effect looking at television use as a tool for understanding family interaction."[16]

The fundamental point which Goodman makes is that previous researchers have tended to concentrate on individual members of the family, rather than studying the family unit as a whole. In the past the research model was often a linear one, in which television was seen to have direct effects on viewers. Things got a little better when people thought in terms of mediation – where, rather than television having direct effects on people, television's effects were seen to be mediated by the family – so that, in effect, the family structure was taken to be a complex of intervening variables, which acted as a filter between the individual and the screen. Where Goodman's work is particularly important is in encouraging us to think about the family's use of television: that is to say, the way in which the family constructs the meaning of television within the home, the ways in which the family members construct their uses of the television set. This is not to deny that television programmes have their own structure, and indeed that television generates a whole set of meanings, rules, values and so on when it enters the home. However, as Goodman notes, "Each family... interprets the set in its own terms, viewing television through its own screen of family rules. It is a kind of family assimilation/accommodation process..."[17]

In many houses the television is kept on continuously, as a kind of "filler" going on continuously behind conversations and domestic events. It will be watched for quick snatches, listened to in moments of quiet and then ignored. Turning off usually signifies a major family tragedy or confrontation.

As Peter Collett of Oxford University puts it: "Television is *what* people talk about, while it is on, as well as at work the next day. It buttresses social relationships in the sense that it gives people something to discuss. Often, it provides a kind of focus for people to talk about other things." Janet Brown, a member of one of the Oxford families filmed by Peter Collett, says:

> "When me and Marie want to have a mother and daughter discussion we will just turn down the television and sit and chat for a couple of hours. I still know what is happening on television, but when I'm having a heart to heart with Marie my sole attention is on her. Actually, a lot of times the programme will actually spark off the discussion. We turn it down so we are watching it *and* having a discussion at the same time."[18]

Goodman's fundamental point is that the family is not just a collection of individuals – it is greater than and different from the sum of its members. Furthermore, she urges us to think about the family in the context of its social *milieu* and in the context of its own life-cycle – that is to say, the "stage of life" of the family, the age of the children and so on. Her fundamental interest is in family processes and her main point is that we should use the family as the unit of analysis and be concerned to understand family processes as they relate to viewing behaviour. Goodman notes that among psychologists studying the family the dining-room table has often served as the focal point for an understanding of family functioning. However, she suggests that given television's acknowledged pervasiveness in the lives of so many families, the family's use of television may well provide us with a better starting-point than their dining-room table behaviour as a key to a better understanding of the way in which the family functions. Her interest is in understanding the ways in which families develop and negotiate rules or principles governing areas of behaviour, and she suggests that this occurs in the field of television viewing as much as anywhere else in the domain of family life. If we looked at the family's eating habits, one might be interested in the way in which the family sits round the table, the rules it has regarding manners, the question of who serves the food, who cooks or prepares it, who carves the meat, what topics of conversation are allowed round the table – all these questions will give us valuable insight into family life. Her suggestion is that if we think about television watching, one can produce equally interesting questions which will likewise allow insights into the way in which the family functions, and into the way in which the family uses television. Her point is that family processes tend to be consistent across different domains of activity. Thus the decision-making processes the family uses in respect of television will probably be similar to those which it uses in relation to other areas of family life. Her point is that given television's central position in the home, rule making, decision making, conflict and dominance in relation to television are naturally major aspects of family process.

Goodman suggests that we look at this situation as one in which we can expect the family to be a rule-governed system whose members behave among themselves in an organised and repetitive manner, and that this patterning of behaviour can be analysed so as to discover the governing principles of family life. This is in respect of family rules of two kinds, both explicit or overt rules, and implicit or covert rules. As she notes, research on the family's uses of television has focused on rules for television viewing, particularly the explicit rules parents may have for the content and quantity of programming that their children are allowed to watch. But, as she notes, these studies are focused on the outcome for the child, rather than the process of rule making. They have not been sensitive to important implicit rules that govern family processes. To understand this, one would have to ask how the rules about television are made in the family, who formulates and who enforces the rules, and whether these rules are simply followed and/or negotiated. As she points out, some rules may be spelled out and well understood by all. Others may be unclear and understood by no one, or only some family members. The prohibition of the specific television programme is a clear rule, but the prohibition of a general category of "unsuitable content" may be difficult to define and enforce. She goes on to note that some implicit rules may revolve around the permissable social interaction of family members when the television set is on. For instance, in some families, watching television is the "OK" time for husband and wife to be in close physical contact, or for other family members to express affection if they have difficulty in doing so at other times. In a family where the members say "We don't have rules about television," she suggests that this simply means that one has to look a little further in order to understand the ways in which implicit rules are operated because, from her perspective, the notion of a family operating without rules of some kind (whether explicit or implicit) is in fact a nonsense. As she points out, television can be used as a controlling mechanism. It can regulate the environment by providing background noise, punctuating time, or scheduling other activities. It can also be used by family members to control one another, or as a means of bartering, as in "I won't watch such and such a programme today if you'll help me do something else." It is hardly uncommon, she suggests, for viewing choices to take the rather displaced form in which someone chooses to watch a certain programme not because they particularly wish to watch that programme, but because they wish to make contact with another member of the family who does want to watch that programme, and watching it together provides a way of having a conversation, having a common talking point.

It is commonly believed that adults use television as a reward or punishment in relation to their children, allowing children to watch television if they are good, or saying to the child, "You can't watch this programme because you didn't eat your greens/clear up your room", or whatever. However, it is also true that adults do this with each other. A husband can use television to get even with his wife in the course of a family dispute simply by watching all the sports events on the television, because he is angry with his wife and knows that watching all this sport will annoy her. Likewise, people can use television in the home to cope with the stresses and strains of the external world. If someone is experiencing dissatisfaction with their job, when they get home they may well not want to interact with other family members. One simple way of achieving this is simply to turn on the television set and "tune out" of the family context.

Goodman also contends that the family is transformed over time – it moves through a number of stages as the children grow up, each of which require restructuring of the family. Thus one can expect television to be used in a variety of ways, depending on the phase of family development, given that television rules and decision-making procedures will need to be constantly revised and updated according to the level of understanding of the children and the needs of the family unit. Clearly, one can't use the same rules for a nine-year-old as one can do when the child is five; or rather, if one does, it is likely to cause conflict within the family!

Of course, it is not simply a question of relationships within the family; one has to think also of the way in which people feel the need to watch certain programmes in order not to be left out at work the next day – if they haven't watched the programme which everyone else is talking about. With children, if all their friends at school habitually watch a certain programme they may well feel that they have to view it if they are not to feel left out by their peer group. Conversely, if the peer-group pressure playing upon adults and children leads them to feel they need to watch different types of programmes, there is then the problem of the parents and children having less common subjects about which to talk. All of this has rather major implications, for instance if we return to the old chestnut concerning the "effects" of violent television programmes on children. If a family uses television to suppress conflict and aggression between family members (that is, retreating into television viewing so as to avoid interaction, which is a fairly common use of television within the home), then this use of television will itself interact with the effects of the programming on the child's behaviour. Thus, to take this one question of the effects of "violent" programming on children's behaviour, one immediately sees that replacing the question within the context of the family as a system, as a process governing and providing a context in which viewing is performed, allows us to approach the question in ways which are much more likely to provide us with adequate answers – or at least to provide us with sensible questions for research.

Television and family interaction

In the same vein Jean Brodie and Lynda Stoneman have developed what they call a "contextualist" framework for studying the influence of television viewing on family interactions.[19] Their interests lie in understanding the ways in which roles within the family interrelate with programme choices and with varieties of response to programme material. Their basic interests lie in the understanding of the contextual variables that determine the salience of television programmes to different members of the family. They are further concerned with the effect of this salience (and therefore the level of interest which different members of the family display towards particular types of television programmes) on the nature of family interactions during different types of programmes. The variables they are concerned with are contextual, such as the question of competing activities in the home, the physical arrangement of the domestic situation; which family members are present; and the specifics of the televisual material which is being viewed at a given time. All these contextual variables, in their view, operate in combination with what they describe as "person variables" (by which they mean the "information processing" skills of the different family members), their roles, their emotional state at a particular time, and so on. Their thesis is that the salience of a television programme is determined by a combination of person and contextual variables and that the salience of a television programme for a family member will determine how much he or she will interact with other family members while that particular programme is being viewed.

As Brodie and Stoneman put it:

"Family members select programmes to view and these programmes in turn serve to organise family interaction. In some cases a television programme will decrease interaction between some family members: in other cases a different programme will increase or maintain family interactions. Thus, the television viewing context actually consists of many contexts, each of which may create different family interaction patterns."[20]

Returning to the question of research that has been done in relation to the effects of television on children, they note that one of the major limitations of much research up to the present has been the focus on the individual child. They note that "little attention has been paid to the possibility that television viewing influences family relations and the socialisation process in the family".[21] In short, they are trying to develop a model of television viewing which is sensitive to the different levels of attentiveness which are paid to the set by different family members in different roles, in relation to different types of programming. They are trying to get away from any notion of the television set simply dominating family life, for all its members in an equal way, whenever it is switched on. They are also trying to get away from the notion that people are either living in their social relations or watching television – as if these two activities were mutually exclusive. Rather, what they are interested in is the way in which the familial roles influence television viewing.

In another piece of research by the same authors, they produce very interesting results about the way in which family interaction varies in relation to different types of programmes. This research established that children were less responsive to other family members during programmes such as cartoon shows. This was not surprising, given that this material addressed them most directly, and most effectively captured their interests. At the same time, they noted that fathers were less responsive to other members of the family during the news. Of considerable interest in relation to my own research was their finding that mothers retained a responsive parenting role across programme types (for details of my own findings in relation to gender-specific type viewing styles, see later). The authors' premise here is that "to the extent that a family member becomes engrossed in a television programme, we would expect that person to initiate fewer interactions with other family members and, in addition, to be less contingently responsive to initiations by others".[22]

Continuing with the theme of gender-specific viewing behaviour, the authors note that family members tend to assume roles that to some extent determine their behaviour in the television viewing context. These authors' findings seem to support the thesis that in family interactions mothers will often assume a "managerial" or "overseer" role, while fathers will assume the "playmate" role in relation to their children – that is, fathers will tend to join their children in activities while mothers sit and monitor the situation. This also applies to the television viewing context. Thus we see again the pattern in which men become engrossed in viewing in a very direct way, which obliterates their concerns with the presence of other members of the family (or rather, that it is much more common for fathers to do this) and that, conversely, it is very uncommon for mothers to assume this position and much more common for them to maintain their managing, supervisory role in the family in relation to all programming. Here these authors are attempting to explain how a perspective can be developed that understands the ways in which family communication in role patterns can explain television use, and can explain the varieties of response to televisual material which are displayed by different family members – precisely in relation to their familial roles. Thus, the authors, quoting research by Brodie, note that "Fathers, while viewing television with their wives and children, tend to become engrossed in the television programme, relying on mothers to enact the parenting role with the children."[23]

What is of further interest here is these authors' understanding of the varied uses to which television can be put. They bring to their analysis an understanding of the very different functions that watching television can perform within the family. Among these functions they note the use of television by parents as a babysitter for fatigued or irritable children, thus providing a way of avoiding the kind of conflict that often arises between parent and child when the child is tired. They also note the not surprising tendency for tired family members to position themselves in front of the television set for long periods of time, only minimally processing the television content, and basically using "watching television" as a way of tuning out input from other family members. This is clearly similar to the incident recounted by Bausinger in the article quoted earlier.

Television can also function as a cause of family conflict. This may arise due to disagreement among family members about what programme to watch, or whether even or not the television set should be on at all. Equally, television viewing may function as a means of escape from family conflict. Brodie and Stoneman quote research that claims to have found a strong relationship between "the amount of time that television sets were reported to be on in a household and self reports of tension and conflict within the family. Thus, it is plausible that television programming can take on increased salience for one or more family members as a mechanism for withdrawing from negative family interaction."[24]

What these authors also point to as a discriminating device is the recognition that most television programming does not demand complete attention. They note that many programmes are designed so that the viewer can engage in other activities, such as conversing with another family member, without missing programme content. However, they note that other programmes require careful attention in order to understand the information being presented. So we have here the recognition that not all television programmes demand the same level of attention, and indeed not all are designed in such a way as to need the same kind of attention from the viewer. As we all know from our own experience, it is perfectly possible to understand the content of many kinds of programmes by means of intermittent listening, or scanty visual attention. One often sees children playing in a room with the television set on and can note that the children monitor the soundtrack of the programme, looking round towards the screen when the soundtrack gives them a clue that something of particular visual interest is about to occur in the programme. Brodie and Stoneman suggest that even by the age of five children have developed "sophisticated strategies for television viewing that allow them effectively to divide their visual attention between television and other competing activities".[25]

So these authors' basic thesis is that the greater the family members' interest in the television programme being viewed, the less they will attend to competing activities and, conversely, the greater their interest in the competing activity, the less they will visually attempt to watch television. Their point, however, is also that this will work in different ways for different family members. As they put it, "the presence or absence of certain perceptual features in the television programme may be accompanied by attention directed toward or away from a programme by various family members. These programme features thereby influence family interaction patterns by commanding the attention of certain family subgroups, diverting attention from interactions with other family members."[26]

Returning to the theme of how people use television in various ways for their own purposes, it is interesting to consider the research of Michelle Wolf, Timothy Mayer and Christopher White.[27] They present a qualitative study of how one particular couple make use of the content of television as a way of constructing conversations between themselves, and with their friends who come round to visit them while they are watching television. As these authors note, this couple, like many others, frequently use television material in order to create topics for talk or to create a common ground with coviewers. In cases such as these, television content is used in order to facilitate conversation, in order to provide themes around which interaction can take place. As they note, this may take the form of conversation running parallel with the programme, commenting directly on television material as it is presented or, indeed, it may be that the television content brings to mind stories, possible anecdotes or jokes which can be "saved up" to be exchanged during the next commercial break, or at the end of the programme. In either case, although these processes may be unconscious, we can reasonably speak of an intentional use of television for the purposes of furthering interaction, rather than once more falling back into the notion of television viewing as an alternative way to social life. These authors are precisely concerned with the ways in which the viewing of television is itself conducted as a social activity. Their concerns are with understanding how television content is used by people to establish and maintain their interpersonal relationships – most often by the way in which television is used to stimulate conversation about past experiences and important day-to-day activities. This may, for instance, take the form of someone being motivated when watching the television to say, "Oh, that reminds me of when . . . ". Here the viewer is using the occasion of television viewing to provide the context in which reminiscences can be exchanged. Or, more argumentatively, it may take the form of the viewers commenting adversely on programme material being viewed – at its simplest, validating each other's sense of themselves as critical viewers, people who will not easily allow the wool to be pulled over their eyes, or people who are aware when they are watching bad acting.

All this is simply to say that one has to understand television watching as something rather more than the individual search either for information or entertainment. That perspective leaves us considering the viewer as an individual consumer, outside of social relations. The perspective being advanced here is one which is precisely interested in the viewers' activities in viewing as part of (and indeed as a constitutive part of) the social and primarily familial or domestic relations through which they construct their lives.

The social uses of television

Another researcher who has investigated the nature of the social uses which audience members make of television is James Lull of the University of California. In his article "The Social Uses of Television",[28] Lull refers back to some previous research conducted by Bechtol in 1972. Bechtol argues that "television viewing does not occur in a vacuum, it is always to some degree background to a complex behaviour pattern in the home ... no doubt an aim of future research is determining the relationship among viewing time, viewing styles, and the larger framework of a family's life-styles".[29] Lull is concerned with the social uses of television, as the title of his article suggests. In particular, he is interested in the ways in which television is used as what he describes as an "environmental resource" – in order to create a flow of constant background noise which moves to the foreground when individuals or groups so desire. As Lull says:

> "TV is a companion for accomplishing household chores and routines. It contributes to the overall social environment by rendering a constant and predictable assortment of sounds and pictures which instantly creates an apparently busy atmosphere. The activated television set guarantees its users a non-stop backdrop of verbal communication against which they can construct their interpersonal exchanges."[30]

What Lull is concerned to investigate is the way in which television viewing contributes to the structuring of the day, punctuating time and family activity – such as meal times, bed times, homework times and so on. His point is that we need to understand the differential times which different members of a family construct for their viewing in relation to their domestic roles and obligations. In particular Lull is concerned with the ways in which television can be used to facilitate communication. He notes that television's characters, stories and themes are employed by viewers as ways of illustrating experience – common references which other people can be expected to understand. As he points out, people often use television pro-grammes and characters as references known in common, in order to clarify issues that they discuss. Television examples are used both by children and adults to explain things to each other – to give the examples and instances which will illustrate the point that someone is trying to make. Within the home, children often use television in order to enter an adult conversation. A child being ignored by several adults talking to each other can gain access to the conversation if he or she can think up an example which illustrates a point being made by one of the people involved in the conversation – very often that example will be drawn from the world of television. In this case the child is using the reference to televisual material as a way of gaining entry to a conversation from which he or she otherwise would have been excluded. More fundamentally, Lull points to the way in which the uneasiness of prolonged eye contact between people can be lessened by the use of the television set, which so ably attracts attention during lulls which occur in conversation. Moreover, the programme being watched at any given point of course creates an immediate agenda for talk where there may otherwise have been none. Thus the medium can be used as a convenient resource for entertaining outside guests in the home. As Lull puts it, "To turn on the set when guests arrive is to introduce instant common ground. Strangers in the home may then indulge in television talk."[31] Thus hosts and guests, in their common role as viewers, can become better acquainted but invest minimal personal risk.

Television viewing is of course something which in many families is precisely done together. In this case the medium can be used to provide opportunities for family members or friends communally to experience entertainment or informational programmnes. To quote Lull again: "A feeling of family solidarity is thus achieved through television – induced laughter, sorrow, anger, or intellectual stimulation."[32] And these forms of interaction may not necessarily be expressed through talk. Other researchers have noted that during the viewing of certain types of programmes, while one *could* come to the conclusion that family interaction is decreased – in the sense that the flow of talk may have dried up (for instance, during the viewing of complex informational programming) – it may well be that while the talking has decreased, the level of touching and other forms of personal intimacy may have increased. That indeed is a fairly common "family rule", that touching or cuddling up together is indeed more common when watching the television with other members of the family than on any other occasion. Indeed, the suggestion that "we should watch the television" may well be one in which the content which we are about to watch could well be the secondary consideration, where the primary consideration may be precisely the opportunity which doing this will provide the family members to sit close together (clearly this does not only apply to family members).

Lull tries to systematise his observations by suggesting that the social uses of television can be understood along two dimensions: the structural dimension and the relational dimension. Along the structural dimension he distinguishes two particular uses: the environmental use (provision of background noise, companionship, and entertainment) and regulative (punctuation of time and activity, talk patterns). On the relational dimension he distinguishes four different social uses. The first of these is what he calls communication facilitation (experience illustration, provision of common ground and agenda for talk, etc.). The second function he refers to is that of affiliation/avoidance (physical, verbal contact, family solidarity). The third is what he calls social learning (which is the use of television for provision of role models, value transmission, all the dissemination of information). The fourth relational use medium which Lull identifies is that of the demonstration of competence or dominance (role enactment, role re-enforcement, gate-keeping). Indeed he goes further, and ends his article by suggesting that it may be possible to construct indices based on these major divisions (especially of the relational uses of television) so as to develop user types and family types. He is suggesting that it may be possible to determine if a particular family predominantly uses television for one or another of the relational functions which he has identified. As he argues, if we could distinguish family types along this dimension (in terms of the predominant use to which they put the television set), one would have gone a long way toward systematising what would otherwise be a complex web of otherwise unaccountable findings.

However, it may be that this typology should itself be used in a different way, which would allow us to see that different families may well engage in various different uses of the television; and far from there being a direct linkage from one family type (which predominantly uses the television set for one or other of the structural or relational uses which Lull has identified), it may rather be the case that any given family uses the television for different purposes at different times, and indeed that different members of the same family may well wish to use the television set for quite different functions.

Lull's own main attempt to extend his work, in terms of this type of systematisation of the social uses of television, is explored in "Family, Communication Patterns and the Social Use of Television".[33] The starting-point of this article is his observation that one factor which influences the way families process television is the nature of the interpersonal communication which takes place in the home.

In this article Lull distinguishes between two types of families. The first of these types is the socio-orientated family, in which parents strongly encourage their children to get along well with other family members and friends, and the child is advised to give in on arguments rather than cause conflict (in my own view, this may have more to do with gender than any other factor). The other family type is the concept-orientated family, where a communicative environment is created in which parents stimulate their children to express ideas and to challenge other beliefs. In general the difference between the family types is the preoccupation in the socio-orientated family with others' feelings, compared with an emphasis in the concept-orientated family with presenting and discussing ideas. Clearly this distinction is not a million miles away from some of Bernstein's formulations of the different socialisation styles of working-class and middle-class families respectively, as laying a basis for the different forms of cultural competence or communicative code (namely, restricted and elaborated code) which Bernstein identifies as characterising these different types of families from these different class backgrounds. Lull's other point is that family members from socio-orientated as opposed to concept-orientated families differ radically in their uses of the mass media. Parents and children in socio-orientated families will tend to have high levels of total television viewing but low levels of news viewing. (Compare this with some of my own findings later.) Conversely, parents and children in concept-orientated families will tend to use the mass media primarily for news and comparatively little for "escape" or entertainment. Concept-orientated family members are also held to have relatively low overall television viewing habits; that is, quite simply, a low level of television consumption. In effect, concept-orientated families are those that value the presentation of personal points of view of the issues under description and do not discourage disagreement or argumentation about these issues. Socio-orientated families, on the other hand, are characterised by an environment where social harmony is prized, and children are told to repress expression of ideas if it would cause interpersonal friction.

However, Lull's attempt to develop this family typology seems to have run into some difficulty. In a later article[34] Lull claims that, not surprisingly, concept-orientated family members view less television, do so more selectively, and are less satisfied with television as a form of family entertainment. However, as he notes:

> "Concept-orientated individuals are also more likely than those with a socio-orientation to report their sensitivity to the needs of others who exist in their interpersonal interaction about programme selection. Further, socio-orientated family members said that arguments about programmes prevailed more often in their homes than did people from concept-orientated households. The conclusion then is that members of socio-orientated families are less sensitive to the needs of others, and more argumentative when television programmes are selected than are individuals from the less harmonious concept-orientated homes."[35]

While the contradictory nature of some of Lull's findings may give us pause when considering the usefulness of the concept-orientated versus socio-orientated family typology, none the less a number of his other findings reported in this particular article are of considerable interest. What Lull investigates here is "Who is responsible for the selection of television programmes at home, how programme selection processes occur, and how the roles of family position and fundamental point at issue here concerns the fact that viewing is often non-selective. That is to say that viewers often watch programmes that are selected by someone else in the family. This is often referred to as "enforced viewing", hardly an uncommon situation in any context in which there is more than one person involved in the viewing group! The point is that programme selection decisions often are complicated interpersonal communication activities involving inter-family status relations, temporal context, the number of sets available and rule-based communications conventions.

Here we approach the central question of power. And within any patriarchal society the power at issue will necessarily be that of the father. This perspective involves us in considering the ways in which familial relations, like any other social relations, are also and inevitably power relations. Lull's central finding, in his survey of control of the television set, was that fathers were named most often as the person (or one of the persons) who controlled the selection of television programmes. Children and mothers were more likely to regard fathers this way than were the fathers themselves. Lull found that fathers controlled more programme decisions than any other single family member (or combination of family viewers) and that they were more than twice as likely as their wives to control such decisions. Indeed, fathers were found to act alone on their programme decisions in more than ninety per cent of the cases observed. One of the children was the next most likely to turn the set on (or off) or change the channels. Mothers were observed to be far less involved in the actual manipulation of the set (compare this with my own findings later) than were either their husbands or children. Indeed, mothers were initiators of programme decisions or actions of this type in a very small percentage of cases, and they were less likely than either fathers or children to undertake such actions or decisions alone. In essence, as Lull puts it, "The locus of control in programme selection process can be explained primarily by family position."[37] Thus, to consider the ways in which viewing is performed within the social relations of the family is also, inevitably, to consider the ways in which viewing is performed within the context of power relations and the differential power afforded to members of the family in different roles – whether in terms of gender or in terms of age.

The question of power and gender relations is of particular interest. Lull's work provides us with a picture of male power within the family, in relation to television viewing, which is very much borne out by my own research. His remarks on the extent to which women are disempowered within the relations of television viewing are also strikingly pertinent. Morever this issue relates to the whole field of family relations and indeed raises the further problem of how difficult it is for most women to construct any leisure time space for themselves within the home – any space, that is, in which they can feel free of the ongoing demands of family life. In this connection the work of Janice Radway on women's reading of romance fiction provides us with a number of helpful parallels. Essentially Radway's research discovered that many of the women she interviewed connected their reading of romance fiction with their rare moments of privacy from the endless demands of family and work life. In effect, her respondents seemed to feel that romance reading was almost a "declaration of independence", in the sense that in picking up a book the woman was effectively erecting a barrier between herself and the arena of the regular family ministrations. As Radway puts it, "Because husband and children are told 'this is my time, my space, now leave me alone' they are expected to respect the signal of the book and to avoid interrupting. Book reading allows the woman to free herself from her duties and responsibilities and provides a 'space' or 'time' within which she can attend to her own interests and needs."[38] Radway concludes that "Romance reading functions for the woman as a kind of tacit, minimal protest against the patriarchal constitution of women – it enables them to mark off a space where they can temporarily deny the selflessness usually demanded of them."[39]

Radway develops this theme further in a second article "Women Read the Romance – the Interaction of Text and Context". In this article she argues that we need to know not "What the romantic text objectively means... but rather how the event of reading the text is interpreted by the women who engage in it."[40] Radway helpfully reformulates the question of "escapism". This derogatory term has often been applied to the consumption of romance fiction. Clearly "escapism" in this sense is almost inevitably held to be a bad thing – the very term is pejorative. However, once we pose the question of "escapism" in relation to power relations, and specifically in relation to the position of women within heterosexual power relations, this activity begins to acquire a whole different meaning. Indeed in the situation in which many women find themselves, escape would seem to be a rather rational strategy. Radway says:

> "When asked why they read romances, the women interviewed overwhelmingly cite escape or relaxation as their goal. They use the word 'escape' however, both literally and figuratively. On the one hand, they valued their romances highly because the act of reading them literally draws the women away from their present surroundings. Because they must produce the meaning of the story by attending closely to the words on the page, they find that

their attention is withdrawn from the concerns that plague them in reality. One woman remarked, with a note of triumph in her voice, 'My body may be in that room, but I'm not.' These women see their romance reading as a legitimate way of denying a present reality that occasionally becomes too hard to bear."[41]

The women I interviewed often displayed guilt when talking about their pleasures in watching romance or soap opera material on television. Radway's research, because it was concerned with the reading of books rather than the viewing of television, brought to light another dimension of the problem. This is to do with the ways in which, because the reading of books has a generally higher cultural status than the viewing of television, there is a way in which for women in this position reading romance fiction in book form is a more acceptable and legitimate activity than viewing the same kind of material on television. As Radway puts it, "This particular means of escape is better than television viewing for these women, because the cultural value attached to books permits them to overcome the guilt they feel about avoiding their responsibilities. They believe that reading of any kind is, by nature, educational. They insist accordingly that they also read to learn."[42] The learning to which they refer is rather similar to the kind of "social learning" which James Lull identified as one of the functions of television viewing. In Radway's previous article she provides this formulation: "Although the books are works of fiction, the women use them as primers about the world. The romance for them is a kind of encyclopaedia and reading a process of education."[43]

Again, clear parallels can be drawn here between the comments which Radway's respondents make on what they feel they learn about human relations from reading romance fiction and the way in which my own respondents talk about watching soap operas as an activity which is very closely related to their concerns in their own lives with family problems, the progress and difficulty of certain relationships and so on. This perspective dates back originally to the work of Lazarsfeld and Hertzog in the 1940s, who researched the response to soap operas on the part of different women. Lull notes that Lazarsfeld and Hertzog's early studies of soap operas demonstrated that "these melodramas provide practical suggestions for social interaction which are widely imitated by audience members... these imitations may be useful in solving family problems which bear resemblance to difficulties resolved in television dramas. At the very least, television provides an abundance of role models which audience members find socially useful."[44]

These two ways of looking at women's viewing or reading of low status soap opera or romance material are particularly instructive. At its crudest, the woman viewer of *Crossroads* is a familiar object of scorn in contemporary humour. This scornful attitude is also displayed by several of the husbands I interviewed, who denigrate their wives' activities in watching this kind of material precisely as escapism – an indulgence in fantasy which is an improper activity for an adult and, indeed, perhaps even an irresponsible activity. Certainly it is an activity which is held to have very low status. However, if we understand the functions of romance or soap opera viewing as part of a strategy of escapism, which can be seen to be very rational given the position in which many women find themselves and, further, if we understand the ways in which many women use the viewing of these types of material in order to learn more about the problems of social life and relationships, one can see that this activity is itself worthy of something more than scorn.

Radway's work clearly has parallels with that of other commentators on women's viewing habits, such as Tania Modleski,[45] Dorothy Hobson[46] and Charlotte Brunsdon,[47] all of whom have attempted to understand more fully what it is that women are doing when they watch fictional programmes, and why it is that they watch them in the way that they do, and with the degree of attentiveness which they give to them. I can only hope that my own work will go some little way in advancing these arguments further.

Research development: from 'decoding' to viewing context

In this short section I wish to attempt to outline in more detail the ways in which this research represents a continuation of my previous work on the *Nationwide* project. This work has already been subject to some debate.[1] My own concerns in relation to my previous work are threefold and the major problems I would identify are the following: first, the difficulties arising from the fact that the *Nationwide* audience study was conducted by interviewing groups of people outside of their homes – i.e., not in their "natural" domestic viewing context. Second, the problems arising from the fact that the *Nationwide* study perhaps allows too little space for the consideration of the contradictory nature of the "decodings" which the same person may make of different types of programme material. Thirdly, the need which I would see for further refinement of the arguments concerning the relationship between specific genres of material and particular sub-categories of the audience.

Let us take these problems one by one, starting with the question of the viewing context. This is a relatively simple matter in so far as in the *Nationwide* study I recruited groups of individuals for interview in the context either of colleges in which they were studying, or in other public locations where they came together, already constituted as groups. While this approach had the obvious advantages of giving me ease of access to groups of people who already functioned as groups, at the same time this strategy had the disadvantage that I was not talking to people about television in the context in which they normally watch it. The problem is that viewing television is done quite differently in the home as opposed to in public places. Indeed, in her article "The Rules of Viewing Television in Public Places"[2] Dafna Lemish goes some way towards accounting the very different ways in which television is watched outside the home – whether it is a husband watching a football game leaning on a couch which is for sale in a department store while his wife is shopping, or a woman who has lunch in a store cafeteria and watches her favourite soap opera on a set for sale in a shop, or the situation of travellers watching a news programme in the lobby in an airport. All these are quite different contexts for watching television, and the way in which it is viewed in these contexts will be quite different from the way in which it is viewed in the home. As I have already indicated, my own interests are now focused on the *how* of television watching – in the sense of understanding how the process of television viewing is done as an activity. This is to say that I would prioritise the understanding of the process of television viewing (the activity itself) over the understanding of particular responses to particular types of programme material (the level at which the *Nationwide* audience study is pitched). It is for this reason that in this new research project the decision was taken to interview families, as family groups, in their own homes – so as to get a better understanding of the ways in which television is watched in its "natural" domestic context. I would wish to argue that this is the necessary framework within which we must place our understanding of the particularity of individual responses to different types of programming.

Regarding the second problem, that of the contradictory nature of responses which individuals may make to different types of programmes, my concerns are the following. In the *Nationwide* audience survey, parallel to the sense in which the particular, empirically observable groups in the survey are to some extent taken to 'represent' classes, there is a further sense in which the *Nationwide* study might be taken to imply that the responses of the individuals in the group – the particular readings which they generate from these programmes in this context – might be taken to "represent" their fundamental, or essential, positions with respect to the totality of cultural practice. Thus, if a shop steward makes an oppositional reading of the *Nationwide* programme on the budget, we might be tempted to assume that this is evidence that the other readings he will make of other programmes in other contexts will similarly display oppositional tendencies.

The question at issue here is clearly closely related to the question raised by all the debates about the positioning of the subject and the contradictory nature of our subject positions. In a review of Ernesto Laclau and Chantal Mouffe's book *Hegemony and Social Strategy*, David Forgacs makes a number of interesting points.[3] As Forgacs explains, Laclau and Mouffe are critical of the essentialist view that individuals and classes are coherent, unified subjects whose actions and consciousness reflect their underlying essence. Against this, Laclau and Mouffe maintain that human subjectivity, far from being the source of people's actions and social relations, is the effect of the latter. They argue that it is only in our social relations that we assume "subject positions", and that, moreover, our subjective identity is multifaceted and "overdetermined". That is to say, it is built up out of many different relations which only partly overlap with one another. For instance, the same man may be simultaneously a productive worker, a trade union member, a supporter of the Social Democratic Party, a consumer, a racist, a home owner, a wife beater and a Christian. Laclau and Mouffe argue that no one of these "subject positions" can be logically derived from any of the others. No one of them is the "essence" underlying the others.

My own view is that while Laclau and Mouffe point to a very important problem, they perhaps go too far in the direction of disaggregating subjectivity – to a point where there is no coherence to be had anywhere. The fact that no one subject position can be logically derived from any of the others does not mean to say that no one of these subject positions is in fact more powerful or more generative than another. The fact that all these subject positions may be logically on the same plane does not mean to say that they are necessarily, empirically, all equivalent. It remains possible that some of these subject positions will be more powerful than others and indeed some may be dependent on others. Thus I would not want to go overboard for a position which assumed that people will be likely to produce totally unconnected "readings" or decodings of cultural objects in different contexts, in so far as this would be to assume that basic structural factors could be totally obliterated by contextual variations. However, we do need to tread carefully here.

Perhaps this issue can be made clearer if we take a hypothetical white male working-class shop steward (identified in the *Nationwide* project) and follow him home, and look at how he might react to another *Nationwide* programme, this time in his home context. First, it would seem likely that in his domestic context, away from the supportive/regulative mores of the group of fellow shop stewards with whom he viewed the "News" tape in the *Nationwide* interview, the intensity of his "oppositional" readings will be likely to diminish. But let us also look at how he might respond to a few items in this hypothetical *Nationwide* on different topics. So, his working-class position has led him to be involved in trade union discourses and thus, despite the weaker frame supplied by the domestic context, he may well still produce an oppositional reading of the first item – on the latest round of redundancies. However, his working-class position has also tied him to a particular form of housing in the inner city, which has, since the war, been transformed before his eyes culturally by Asian immigrants, and the National Front come closest to expressing his local chauvinist fears about the transformation of "his" area; so he is inclined to racism when he hears on the news of black youth street crimes – that is to say, he is getting close to a dominant reading at this point. But then again his own experience of life in an inner city area inclines him to believe the police are no angels. So when the next item on the programme turns out to be on the Brixton riots he produces a negotiated reading, suspicious both of black youth and also of the police. By now he tires of *Nationwide*, and switches over to a situation comedy in which the man and woman occupy traditional positions, and his insertion within a working-class culture of masculinity inclines him to make a dominant reading of the programme . . .

So, we have here a person making different readings of the same material in different contexts, and making different readings of material on different topics – oppositional in some areas, dominant in others. He is indeed a "subject crossed by a number of discourses", but it is *he*, the particular person (who represents a specific combination of/intersection of such discourses), who makes the readings, not the discourses which "speak" to him in any simple sense. Rather, they provide him with the cultural repertoire of resources with which he works.

This is to stress the point that the Althusserian drift of much early cultural studies work (and it is this which, evidently, underlies much of the *Nationwide* project) would reduce our shop steward to the status of a mere personification of a given structure, "spoken" by the discourses which cross the space of his subjectivity. However, it is not simply Althusser who is at issue here; much of the psychoanalytic work on the theory of ideology generates an equally passive notion of subjectivity, in which the subject is precisely "spoken" by the discourses which constitute that person. I want to try to formulate a position from which we can see the person actively producing meanings from the restricted range of cultural resources which his or her structural position has allowed them access to.

Crudely, this is to argue that there is a tendency in the *Nationwide* book to think of deep structures (for instance, class positions) as generating direct effects of the level of cultural practice. That is a tendency which I would want to qualify more now, to examine in detail the different ways in which a given "deep structure" works itself out in particular contexts, and to try to reinstate the notion of persons actively engaging in cultural practice. To put the point another way, "one cannot conclude from a person's class, race, gender, sexual orientation and so on, how she or he will read a given text (though these factors do indicate what cultural code she or he has access to). It is also a question of how she or he thinks and feels about living her/his social situation."[4] Or, to paraphrase Sartre, it is a question of what we make of what history has made of us.

Let us turn now to the third difficulty – that of the need for further refinements of the theory of the relationships between particular genres or types of material and particular audience subgroups. The work of Armand Matellart[5] in relation to cultural imperialism and the work of Phil Cohen and David Robins[6] on youth culture can perhaps provide models of how we could usefully approach the question both of power (and its limits) and conversely the question of why particular groups seem to be attracted to particular types of cultural material. In an earlier article I noted:

"Matellart argues that the idea that imperialism 'invades' the different sectors of a society in a uniform way has to be abandoned. He proposes that we substitute for that approach a more precise analysis, where particular sectors or *milieux* of a society favour or resist 'penetration' by a range of different, particular ideological forms. If we transfer the logic of that argument to the narrower national context we can then relate Matellart's fundamental point to Cohen and Robins' work on youth culture. Cohen and Robins are concerned to explain the specific popularity of one genre of text (kung fu movies) among one section of the society – urban/working class/male/youth. Their argument is that the genre is popular precisely to the extent that it 'fits' with the forms of cultural competence available to this group."[7]

As argued in that article, this perspective is clearly related to the work of Bourdieu on the distribution of different forms of cultural competence within different parts of the social structure. I would in fact argue that this current research project has allowed me to develop the comments made in the closing pages of the article cited above about the ways in which both soap opera and current affairs television appeal to specific "publics" (in these cases defined both by gender and by class). The point made in that article is that each of these forms of television requires the viewer to be competent in certain forms of knowledge, and to be familiar with certain conventions which constitute the ground (or framework) within or on which particular propositions can be made. The further point is that these are forms of cultural competence which are unevenly distributed within our society. At its crudest, some people in each case simply do not possess the forms of cultural competence which are necessary in order to understand and gain pleasure from the viewing of these particular types of materials. These are facts which are determined outside of the sphere of television – by family socialisation and by education. I would suggest that one of the main points of interest in this current research is the evidence that is generated about the ways in which particular types of material can be seen to appeal particularly strongly to particular sub-sections of the audience.

However, there is a further problem with the *Nationwide* project, which concerns the relative weight given in that research to understanding the responses which individuals make to types of material which can be shown to them, as against the weight given to understanding which types of material they might see as relevant to them in the first place. To understand this we need to deal more directly with the relevance/irrelevance and comprehension/incomprehension dimensions of interpretation and decoding, rather than being directly concerned with the acceptance or rejection of particular substantive ideological themes or propositions. This is, of course, the fundamental limitation of the encoding/decoding model as derived from Parkin's work[8] – in so far as this framework almost inevitably leads to a focus precisely on the question of whether a particular proposition is decoded in a dominant, negotiated or oppositional way. In retrospect, it seems to me that many of the responses which different groups in the *Nationwide* audience survey make to particular programme items need to be seen in the context of a perspective which would recognise that, for many of those groups, they would simply not have been watching the programme in the first place; or that if they had been in the room when the programme was on they would not have been watching this particular item in the programme. In short, what we have at the end of the *Nationwide* project is a series of responses to material which is not necessarily salient to the respondents. In effect, we only have an account of their decodings of this material because it was artificially supplied to them. The more interesting question perhaps is precisely that of which kinds of material they would be interested in watching and, which kinds of material they would not watch. Clearly the question of whether they would make a dominant, negotiated or oppositional reading of a certain type of programme material is less relevant than the question of whether or not they would choose to watch that type of material in the first place. In this connection Lindloff and Traudt quote from the work of Bloomer, who provides a useful scenario for thinking about the interpretive procedures standing between the individual user and the mass media. As Bloomer says:

> "Their interests, their forms of receptiveness, indifference, or opposition, their sophistication or naivity, and their established scheme of definition set the way in which they initially receive the presentation. Usually there is a further intervening stage before the residual effects of the presenta-

tions are set in experience and behaviour. This additional stage is an interpretive process which, through analysis and critical judgement, reworks the presentations into different forms, before assimilation into experience. This process of interpretation in the individual is markedly guided by the stimulations, cues, suggestions, and definitions he secures from other people, particularly those constituting his so called 'reference groups'. Account must be taken of the collective process of definition which, in different ways, shapes the manner in which individuals composing the 'audience' interpret and respond to the presentations given through the mass media."[9]

The point here, from my own perspective, lies in the relative weight to be given to the remarks at the beginning of the quote about forms of receptiveness or indifference. As I have already suggested, it may well be that this is the fundamental question to be explored, rather than the question of what interpretation people will make of a given type of programme material if they are specifically put in a room and asked to make an interpretation. It is this thread of inquiry which the current research project has attempted to explore. And it is for this reason that the question of the pertinence or salience of different types of programme material to different family members or to members of families from different social backgrounds has been prioritised in this research above the question of their tendency to make oppositional, negotiated or dominant readings or interpretations of particular types of programme material.

Relation to other research

This project was specifically designed to complement two other particular pieces of research: the BBC's recent study of leisure time activity[10] and Peter Collett's study of viewing behaviour conducted at Oxford Polytechnic.[11]

The project attempted to pursue a number of the issues raised by the findings of the BBC's time-budget study. That study presents us with a wealth of detail on patterns of leisure activity. However, my objective was to investigate the reasons people give for making the leisure choices they make. My premise was that it is only within the context of a perspective which sees the family as the "unit of consumption", rather than the individual viewer, and which investigates both the internal dynamics of the family and wider set of social and cultural determinants in which the family is located, that we shall be able to begin to understand why people make the leisure/viewing choices that they do.

The "Daily Life" study represents a significant attempt to provide an overall map of the changing patterns of leisure activity, by means of large-scale survey work. This project was designed to explore the qualitative questions which lie behind the quantitative patterns thus revealed: why certain media/programme types are chosen by different kinds of viewers; how those choices are made within the social relations of the family; how/why people respond in particular ways to the material which they view.

This project was also designed to complement the work being done at Oxford by Peter Collett and his colleagues on the actual behaviour of families in front of their television set. That work is clearly of great interest in providing us with a full picture of the complexity of actual recorded behaviour at times when respondents might simply report that they had been "watching television". Collett's work decisively shifts the ground of much debate about the television audience, not least by simply confirming what we all know from the evidence of our own living-rooms – that watching television in the family home is a very complex process in which the kind of attention which different people pay to different types of programming, at different time of the day varies enormously. Or, as Bob Towler of the Independent Broadcasting Authority put it in his presentation to the Royal Television Society, "availability plays an important part in determining presence, and then... presence means a hundred things".[12] The tapes made by Collett show the families concerned engaging in an almost bizarre variety of different activities: we eat dinner, knit jumpers, argue with each other, listen to music, read books, do homework, kiss, write letters and vacuum-clean the carpet with the television on. As Collett says, "People spend hours on end doing all kinds of things that have absolutely nothing to do with TV viewing while the set is on."

It is of considerable interest to compare the accounts given by the families in my sample of how they view with the patterns of behaviour revealed by Collett's work. While some part of the accounts which people give of their behaviour can doubtless be categorised as rationalisation, that need not be taken to mean that such accounts cease to be of interest. Rather, it presents us with a valuable opportunity both for investigating the bases of the important variables between the accounts given by different viewers, and for investigating further the relationships between what people understand themselves to be doing, and what the video camera seems to show them to be doing.

Besides the two pieces of contemporary research referred to above, this project also has implications for one other body of work in particular – that of Ehrenberg and Goodhart, whose account of the "random" nature of much viewing behaviour has come to be accepted as "trade wisdom" over the last few years.[13]

I argued earlier that the category "watching television" was so indiscriminate as to produce misleading research data, and that what is important is to discover the significant variations (of attention, interest and response) which are concealed by this "catch-all" category. I further want to argue that Ehrenberg and Goodhart's work tends to blur these differences and that my results raise serious questions about Ehrenberg *et al.*'s basic thesis, in so far as my respondents demonstrate considerable degrees of consistency in their stated programme preferences and in their accounts of the concomitant variations in levels of attention paid to different types of programming. I recognise that I am working with people's accounts of their television viewing, rather than with direct records of their behaviour. None the less, this evidence is strong enough for me to hypothesise that my findings would be replicated by behavioural research conducted within the framework that I have outlined.

In essence, my argument is that Ehrenberg *et al.* move improperly from the observation that stated programme/channel preference is no direct predictor of actual behaviour to the conclusion that it is of little relevance. I would argue that these factors remain of considerable relevance, but that they need to be understood in the context of the competing demands of work, domestic and social obligations, which will always inflect the effectivity of programme preferences but should not be understood to negate them. In short, having previously argued[14] that the critical formula was that of a programme's ideological problematic plus its mode of address (in relation to audience "tastes", cultural capital and political views), I now want to extend that formula to include a third term, which is that of audience "availability" (both in terms of physical presence and freedom from competing demands on attention). One example of this is to be found in the interview with F15 (see below).

In that interview, the couple's comments on the way in which what they watch is determined (both positively, in the case of *Miami Vice*, and negatively, in the case of *Crossroads*) by the interaction of two factors (time availability and programme taste) are instructive in advancing us beyond the widely accepted interpretation of Ehrenberg's work. Ehrenberg is careful to say that stated programme preferences and actual viewing behaviour are quite different things. However, his work has largely been taken to imply that because stated programme preferences are not good predictors of actual viewing behaviour, therefore they are of little account. My own view, which I believe is supported by the findings in this survey, is that we need to develop a theory of the complex ways in which programme preferences are translated (through their intersection and interaction with other factors, such as domestic and work obligations) into viewing behaviour. Clearly, preferences do not directly predict behaviour – that is, they are not a sufficient condition of viewing behaviour. However, they do need to be seen as a necessary condition of (attentive) viewing behaviour. The issue is to understand which other conditions are also necessary for viewing behaviour to result – that is, what is the combination of necessary causes and conditions that will constitute a sufficient cause. Put another way, rather than thinking in mono-causal terms and rejecting the relevance of a factor which does not, by itself, cause the effect we are interested in, we should think in terms of an overdetermined (or multifactorial) theory of causality.

Set in this context, this couple's responses are of considerable interest. The woman explains that she watches *Miami Vice* because of the positive correlation of "preference" and "availability". "*Miami Vice* – Yes I watch that a lot. It's quite a good one, that is, and that's on at a time when I'm usually coming in, so I can watch that." Conversely, she doesn't watch *Crossroads* because of the negative correlation of these two same factors: "It's on, but we never really take it in. We used to watch it – the telly's on for that but it's not really... I find it a bit boring, actually – it seems to have lost its... and it's the time the kids are getting ready for bed. You're half and half watching it. We don't bother hardly at all, but it's still on."

My argument is that viewed from this perspective a considerable degree of sense can be imparted to what otherwise appear as either contradictory and self-cancelling (or insignificant) statistical patterns in terms of variations in viewing choices, behaviour, attention and response.

4
Objectives, methodology and sample design

As I have already stated, this research project was designed to investigate the changing uses of television among a sample of families of different types, drawn from a range of social positions. It was designed to investigate, in terms of the differences between families in different social positions and between families with children of different ages:

(a) the increasingly varied uses of the household television set(s) – for receiving broadcast television, video games, teletext; etc.;

(b) patterns of differential 'commitment' and response to particular types of programming;

(c) the dynamics of television use within the family: how viewing choices are expressed and negotiated within the family; the differential power of particular family members in relation to viewing choices at different times of the day; the ways in which television material is discussed within the family;

(d) the relations between television watching and other dimensions of family life: television as a source of information on leisure choices; leisure interests and work obligations (both inside and outside the home) as determinants of viewing choices.

The project was designed to identify and investigate the differences hidden behind the catch-all description "watching television". We all "watch television", but with how much attention and what degrees of commitment and response, in relation to which types of programming, in which scheduling spots? In pursuing this line of investigation I was aiming to lay the groundwork for the development of a set of culturally differentiated "appreciation indexes", which would accommodate the varied patterns of taste and response as between different sub-sectors of the audience.

Moreover, as argued earlier, we are now in a situation where watching broadcast television is only one among various possible uses of the domestic television set. Among the questions I set out to explore were the following ones. Which family members, in which types of families use their televisions for which of these purposes at which points in the day? What are the factors which give rise to these different patterns, and how are they understood by respondents themselves? Further, how are the differing priorities and preferences of different family members negotiated and resolved in relation to conflicting demands on the use of the television, and within that framework, about particular viewing preferences? In short, how do family dynamics interact with viewing behaviour? These are some of the questions which this pilot project was designed to investigate, in the belief that they represent key issues which broadcast research needs to confront.

Methodology

This pilot project aimed to pursue the problems facing broadcasters in relation to the questions outlined above, and thus clarify the problems which will need to be resolved in later survey research. For this reason the methodology adopted was a qualitative one, whereby each family was interviewed in depth in order to elucidate their (various) accounts of how they understood the role of television in their overall leisure activities. By this means, the aim was to gain insight into the terms within which our respondents themselves defined their viewing activities. Centrally, I aimed thus to generate insights into the criteria used by viewers in making choices and in responding (positively or negatively) to different types of programming and scheduling. I believed that this approach would produce some insights into the criteria lying behind (and generating) particular responses and viewing choices. Thus it was hoped that the project would provide a useful complement to the results of survey work which itself, while usefully detailing the overall pattern of viewing choices made, cannot hope to explain why these choices and responses are made.

Eighteen families were interviewed in their own homes during the spring of 1985. Initially the two parents were interviewed, then later in each interview their children were invited to take part in the discussion along with their parents. The interviews, which lasted between one and two hours, were tape-recorded and then transcribed in full for analysis.

The fact that the interviews were conducted *en famille* doubtless means that respondents felt a certain need to play out accepted roles, and doubtless interviews with family members separately would bring out other responses. However, I was precisely interested in how they functioned *as families*, within (and against) their roles.

Moreover, the interviewing method (unstructured discussion for a period between one and two hours) was designed to allow a fair degree of probing. Thus on points of significance I returned the discussion to the same theme at different stages in the interview, from different angles. This means that anyone "putting me on" (consciously or unconsciously) by representing themselves through an artificial/stereotyped *persona* which has no bearing on their "real" activities would have to be able to sustain their adopted *persona* through what could be seen as quite a complex form of interrogation! Nonetheless, it remains true that I am dealing ultimately with respondents' accounts of what they do. As already indicated, there were a number of built-in safeguards in my interviewing technique against the possibility of respondents offering entirely untruthful accounts of their viewing behaviour (not to mention the safeguard provided by the presence of other members of the family who often chipped in with their own queries when their husbands or wives seemed to them to be misrepresenting their activities).

These considerations are perhaps of particular relevance to the later analysis of "TV and Gender", where readers may feel that respondents' accounts offer a more sharply stereotyped representation of gendered viewing behaviour than is borne out by their own experience – for instance, in relation to the marked tendency for men to claim to be almost exclusively interested in factual programming. Even if it could be successfully argued that my results misrepresent the actual viewing behaviour of these men, it would remain a social fact of considerable interest that these were the particular accounts of their behaviour that these viewers felt constrained to give.

Sample design

The sample consisted of eighteen families. All were drawn from one area of South London. All possessed a video recorder. All consisted of households with two adults living together with two or more dependent children, up to the age of eighteen. All were white. Within this standardised framework, the sample was divided so as to allow for comparisons and contrasts between families in different social positions and families with children at different ages.

The limitations of my budget meant that it was only possible to have a very small sample, all recruited within one quite small, geographical area. The effects of this budgetary limitation meant that my results provide what I would hold is a true and valid picture not of the UK population's viewing habits as a whole (for one thing, all my sample are traditional nuclear families, which in fact represent only a minority of UK households) but of white working-class/lower middle-class families in a stable inner city environment. This represents the limits of the generalisability of my findings.

The particularity of my sample can be specified quite simply. One notable point is that because of the nature of the area where respondents were recruited, I have a very high proportion of working-class/lower middle-class families – not necessarily in terms of income (my sample includes quite a wide range of income) but in terms of all the other aspects of class (cultural capital, education, etc.). Thus my B/C1 respondents are builders who have "made good" rather than educated professionals. The absence of this category of people from my sample is one of its most obvious limitations, and derives quite simply from the fact that the area from which the sample was drawn has not yet been gentrified to any large extent. Another limitation is indexed by the fact that the population of the area is very stable. Many of the families in my sample have lived there all their lives (and often their parents before them), therefore they are a particularly stable group geographically with strong roots in their local community; hence their particularly strong and favourable responses to programmes such as *Only Fools and Horses*, set in the working-class areas of London with which they identify.

Conversely, the geographically mobile (no doubt, as a group, partly co-extensive with the professional/educated category referred to above) are absent from my sample. Doubtless my findings would be very different with a sample recruited from the professional, geographically mobile "non-nuclear" viewers of a more up-market area.

All this has an obvious bearing on the strength of the gender differentiation within the families in my sample. I am not arguing that all families in the United Kingdom repeat this pattern. Indeed, I would be amazed if it was repeated among more highly educated professional families. However, I am claiming that gender differentiation and very traditional sex role stereotyping is very strong among working-class/lower middle-class families in stable inner city areas, and that among families of this type this has all the consequence which I refer to later in terms of viewing patterns.

Table 1

Sample Details

	Family	Family Income	Job (Head of Household)	Age left Education (HoH)	Home Status	Years in Residence	Holidays in last year	Political Preference	Approximate Age of youngest child
B	F16	£11k	Builder(S-E)	19yrs	Owner	8½	1	Con	6
	F11	£12k	Manager	18yrs	Owner	10	1	Lab	6
	F8	£15.5k	Carpenter/Builder(S-E)	15yrs	Owner	18	1	Con	12
	F4	(?)	Furniture Dealer	19yrs	Owner	10	1	?	18
C_1	F9	£16.5k	Salesman (S-E)	15yrs	Owner	11	1	Lab	12
	F14	£11.5+	Caretaker	16yrs	Owner	1¼	1	Con	6
	F15	£17k	Decorator (S-E)	16yrs	Tenant	1½	2	Lab	6
C_2	F17	£12k	Fitter	17yrs	Tenant	10	1	Lab	12
	F13	£12k+	Caretaker	15yrs	Tenant	10	3	Lab	12
	F18	£7.5k+	Builder (S-E)	15yrs	Tenant	3	2	Con	18
	F12	£13k	B Telecom Technician	15yrs	Owner	20	2	?	18
	F10	£10k	Postman	17yrs	Tenant	2	3	Lab	6
	F7	£8k	Service Engineer	14yrs	Owner	28	6	Lab	12
U	F6	u	Ex-builder	16yrs	Tenant	13	0	Lab	18
	F5	u	Ex-ambulance worker	14yrs	Tenant	17	1	Con	18
	F3	u	Ex-landscape gardener	15yrs	Tenant	7	0	Lab	6
	F2	u	Ex-decorator	15yrs	Tenant	5	1	Ecol	18
	F1	u	Ex-caretaker	16yrs	Tenant	¾	0	Lab	6

Notes:

1. The class categorisations have been made by means of what is, in the end, an intuitive judgement, whereby class is assessed as a factor of income × educational background × cultural capital × home status. A simple income calculation would produce a different categorisation. I am using the standard ABC, etc., classifications merely as a descriptive short-hand to give a rough indication of class position.

2. The sample is, unfortunately, rather restricted at the top end of the scale. It lacks any substantial representation of the higher educated, professional classes.

Table 2

	Sample by age of children		
	Youngest child: 0-6	**6-12**	**12-18**
B	F16 F11	F8 F4	
C$_1$	F14 F15	F9	
C$_2$	F10	F7 F13 F17	F12 F18
U	F1 F3		F2 F5 F6

Note:
Although the sample was recruited on the basis of age of *eldest* child in family, it subsequently became clear that the age of the *youngest* child in the family is the more important determinant for our purposes and the sample has been recategorised (as above) on this latter basis for analytical purposes.

Table 3

	Number of televisions (colour and black and white)	Video	Teletext
F1	1c	yes	no
F2	1c + 1 b/w	yes	no
F3	1c + 1 b/w	yes	yes
F4	3c + 1 b/w	yes	no
F5	1c	yes	no
F6	1c + 1 b/w	yes	no
F7	1c + 2 b/w	yes	no
F8	1c + 2 b/w	yes	no
F9	1c + 1 b/w	yes	no
F10	2c + 2 b/w	yes	yes
F11	1c + 1 b/w	yes	no
F12	1c + 1 b/w	yes	no
F13	1c + 1 b/w	yes	no
F14	1c	yes	no
F15	1c + 1 b/w	yes	yes
F16	1c	yes	yes
F17	1c + 1 b/w	yes	no
F18	1c + 1 b/w	yes	no

5

Family interviews

(i) Unemployed families

Family 1

This couple are both twenty-seven years old with a boy aged five and
a girl aged two. Both husband and wife left school at sixteen. He is an
unemployed ex-caretaker; she does childminding at home for other
mothers in their street. They are tenants in a large council estate and
have lived in this area for some years, near to their relatives. They are
both Labour voters. Their flat is quite shabby and their possessions
are few. They rent one colour television set and a video (which they
are now tempted to return, given their financial difficulties) and
haven't had a holiday in the last twelve months.

The woman does childminding at home and she uses the television
and video a great deal to help amuse the children during the day. In
fact, their television is on all day, from TV-am in the morning: "My
reaction at the start of the day is to put it on, and I might as well not.
Sometimes I intend to look at it ... but it's so early in the morning ...
at the end of it I've seen everything but I've heard nothing. You know
what I mean?" As the woman puts it, they watch television: "quite a
lot, yeah. Well I put it on for stuff in the mornings because ... well, I
do childminding. I've a child who comes from the children's centre
likes to watch television. She's just here by herself. She watches then,
and it's on in the afternoon, and it's on for children's TV and it just
stays on then. Then they go to bed and we watch it – but it's mainly on
because of the kids."

Clearly she worries a little about how much time the children
spend watching television but it "helps a lot" to have that to "keep
them quiet", and she does feel that some programmes are "good for
them". "Well, for the kids it's virtually the same thing day in, day out
and we have the television on anyway. I mean, they're quite interested
in television and sometimes they look at it so much that you wouldn't
know if it's good for them or not. Well, they tend to sit and just stare
at it, you know. Yes, it's nice to keep them quiet but ... it is distracting
them occasionally ... it helps a lot ... and some of the programmes
are good for them actually."

Moreover, she is conscious of her responsibilities as a childminder and is at pains to point out that she is selective about what she allows the children to watch – especially in relation to "violence". She explains that when she herself watched *Knightrider*, "I was quite surprised and didn't let them watch it any more. There's a lot of violence in it. Some people don't seem to mind if their kids watch things like that. You'd be amazed at the people who let their kids watch some of these video films that are horrible. I don't think it can do them any good at all... the violent parts, you know, they go copying it out on their friends. That's how they grow up – I don't think that can do them any good."

Her husband takes a slightly different view of the matter, feeling that children are not simply affected by programmes in this way: "Well, I don't think they can understand it all... I think they understand what they want to understand. They paint their own pictures, so to speak. They twist it round." But it is, after all, his wife rather than him who has the responsibility in this matter, and hence her views prevail.

As for the couple's own viewing habits, the wife is again anxious to distinguish them from people who simply have their television "blaring" all the time. If people come round this couple turn it down. For instance, "if we invite people to come up for dinner – like if my mum and dad came up – I do think TV interrupts. I think it does stop things at times... I mean, you have a chat and suddenly the TV takes over." This approach is something which she clearly feels to be quite important – and contrasts with her own sister's family, for example. "If I go down to my sister's house, it's blaring, absolutely blaring, but no one is actually watching it, nobody will turn it down. You're actually shouting across to one another. I say, 'Can you just turn it down a bit?' 'Oh yeah, yeah,' they say. Our television would stay all day at that volume – if it were left to the children. They never turn it up or down, whether they are stone deaf or not, I don't know!! It's literally blaring, blaring."

In fact this woman would often prefer to listen to the radio for relaxation rather than have the television on, but she gives in usually to her children's and husband's desire to watch television: "Actually, in the evening if there's nothing on television – or if he's out, if there's some nice, what you call 'classical' music – I like to sit and listen to that. Yes, if they've gone to bed and I just want peace and quiet, you know, to relax to. I haven't done it for a while, actually. The television is on so much, it tends to get to you after a while. The thing is, the kids like the television on so much. In the mornings I might prefer the radio on – we don't listen to a lot of radio – I might put the radio on and it's 'Oh Mum, put the telly back on,' you know."

In terms of channel preferences, their main interest (especially the woman) is in Independent Television. As the woman said, "We tend to watch ITV more – well, I do," whereas her husband qualified this by noting that "sometimes I like the documentaries on BBC." Clearly, channel preference is closely allied with programme type preference, and each channel is identified in their minds with a particular programme type.

This couple claim to have reasonably complementary programme tastes and say that they have very few conflicts over programme choice that cannot be resolved by recourse to videoing the other's preferences (except when the husband insists on seeing live sport "because I'm keyed up for that time to see it". As the husband puts it, noting as an exception one common area of gender conflict ("zany comedy"): "We've virtually got the same taste, apart from the *Young Ones*, I really like that. She hates it."

However, it is clear that their basic preferences do incline in different directions (for her, fiction and soap opera in particular; for him, sport and some wildlife documentaries) and fall within the predominant pattern of gender stereotyping in the sample. When asked which programmes they'd each make a point of being in to watch attentively, the woman gives *Dallas* as the key example and the man replies, "Sports, darts and things like that. Snooker. I like that. Any sport – I like any kind of sport..." The husband does in fact share his wife's interest in *Coronation Street*, which they watch and talk about together, but beyond this he wryly, and perhaps a little defensively, admits to being a rather uninterested and incompetent viewer of soap opera. "I've been sitting down watching *Dallas* and waiting for something to happen that happened in *Dynasty*, you know. But both of them, they're virtually based on the same theme. I get fed up with it after a bit." On these occasions his wife has to come to the rescue: "I tend to keep him up with it." Although she doesn't watch *Crossroads* ("It's the busy time of the evening") or *Brookside*, soap opera is a substantial topic of conversation with her women friends. She finds that she often talks about *Dynasty*.

"Actually, my mum and my sister don't watch it and I often tell them bits about it. If my sister watches it, she likes it – and I say to her, 'Did you watch?' and she says, 'No.' If there's something specially good on one night – you know, you might see your friends and say, 'Did you see so-and-so last night?'... I occasionally miss *Dynasty*, and I've said to a friend, 'What happened?' and she's caught me up, but I tend to see most episodes. Marion used to keep me going, didn't she, about what was happening."

This couple also replicate the pattern in my findings where the woman is quite happy about the fantasy element of watching soap opera (and American soap opera in particular) while the man disapproves strongly of this form of "escapism": The wife says of *Dynasty*: "That's what's nice about it. It's a dream world, isn't it?" Whereas her husband takes the opposite view and complains that "It's a fantasy world that everyone wants to live in. But that – no, I can't get on with that." Moreover, for him, this anti-escapist/pro-realist criterion not only works to discriminate between programme types, but also within particular programmes. "*Crossroads*? No, I don't like it. I don't like any of the characters. I used to like Benny. I liked him. He seemed the only one true to life, you know, but the rest of them are just make-believe."

One other point of relatively clear difference in programme tastes concerns *Widows* – about which the wife is very enthusiastic, saying that it is "the sort of thing that I always follow up". By contrast her husband says, "Well, I'm not a great lover of it. No, I'm not. I watched it a couple of times. They seem too masculine. I watched it. It was very good, you know, but ... as I say – if I'm here, I watch it, but..."

In a number of other ways this couple also conform to classic gender patterns as far as viewing preferences are concerned. In terms of films the woman opts for musicals (for instance, *Flashdance*) and the man for "things like James Cagney". He is a regular viewer of the weekend programme "all about cars and woodwork, and things like that" and she is a fan of Delia Smith. Similarly, he likes horror films, while his wife (like most other women in the sample) dislikes them intensely because of their violence: "To me they're just, I don't know, very violent. I mean, there's enough violence in the world without having to sit and watch it. OK, they've got good stories, some of them. Occasionally I might watch one, but more often than not I think, 'Oh, I'll go up to bed and he can watch it'."

Interestingly, here the standard pattern of my findings seems to be reversed – it is the woman who is more interested in news and current affairs programming and the man who is totally alienated from what he sees as the "pointless" forms of politics which dominate the news. He just "gets fed up with it" (political news, that is) and is utterly cynical in this respect: "I get fed up reading it in the papers. It's on the television, it's on the radio. You've got your own outlook, haven't you? But no one's got a great say other than the politicians, have they? Once they have made their minds up and it's gone through Parliament you've got no choice, so what you read is a lot of propaganda." However, interestingly, he makes an exception for *Weekend World*, which he does like, precisely because he feels that programme's irreverent style of presentation pierces through the politicians' propaganda: "I tell you what I did watch, on a Sunday –

Weekend World. That was really good. I did like that, and that was really mostly about politics. Actually, that is a bit like *Question Time* in the way it tends to really get to the point of things. If he [the interviewer] really wants to dig into them [the politicians], he does."

The man's only other interest in documentary programming is in "some of the wild animal documentaries". By contrast, his wife likes the daytime *Sarah Kennedy* programmes (like some of the other women in the sample), because she "gets an audience and a subject, say, football hooliganism. They have quite good subjects on there sometimes. I'm quite interested if I can hear it." She also likes *Question Time*, although she says that her husband is "not so keen" on it. As far as she is concerned, *Question Time* is good because "I'm interested in what they say. I listen to every word. I think there is for and against with everything, and on there I think they listen to people's points and I suppose it's because they ask questions you'd like to ask, and therefore you're listening to them. They definitely get some good points."

Her husband, unlike her, has a strong interest in comedy programmes – the *Young Ones*, and *Only Fools and Horses* in particular: "The things I follow are – I like any comedy things. I love comedy – anything like that I really do like. I like *The Young Ones*. Some of the comedy programmes, I watch a lot of them. I like *Only Fools and Horses...* the two of them go so well together, as brothers... they're believable, they're true to life ... yes, very true to life."

However, at the same time he clearly feels that comedy is one thing and crime series are quite another. Hence his disappointment at what he perceives as the increasing input of comic elements (over "action") in *Minder*: "I like *Minder*, but I think they go over the top now. It's gone on too long – the humour's starting to die out a bit. Where before they used to – Terry, his name is – you used to see him fight and everything, now, I can't remember the last time I've seen him fight on there. Every week there used to be a grand finale where he'd beat four or five blokes up. There's no more of that now, there's more humour now. And even though I like humour, I don't like seeing a programme go from one thing to another. I'd rather it was based on that one thing."

Beyond this, his great love is sport – and darts in particular. As a player himself, this was also one of the main motivations for him getting a video: so he could tape, rewatch and study the darts matches in order to improve his own darts technique: "I especially wanted to get it because of the darts, I definitely wanted to tape the darts and have a real good look, you know... I had one tape that was specifically darts and nothing else. I used to tape all the darts matches. I would play the same match, time and time again. With kids, now I can't turn professional. It's done me a lot of good, when I look at it and I see what numbers they are going for and how they do a finish, I can see exactly how they do it, slow it down and study it, like a jockey would look at a video of a race and footballers would do."

The other thing the husband enjoys is making subversive readings of what he sees as "snobby" quiz shows: "I used to like *Mastermind*. I haven't got a clue what they're on about though I answered a question one week! My idea about *Mastermind* is to tape it, look at it everyday, and when somebody comes in, put it on, you know, 'ssh!' and you start answering the questions! See what I mean! Lovely, yeah! 'Christ, it was easy this week!' The times we used to watch *Mastermind*, I was waiting for somebody to crack up."

Interestingly, in terms of the gender-determined preferred modes of viewing established in my sample, the man also has a strong preference for going to the cinema, rather than watching films on video (which being unemployed he can't, in fact, indulge). As he explains, what he likes is that the cinema involves a more attentive and concentrated form of viewing: "If I had the choice of using a tape or going to the pictures, I think I'd go to the pictures, because you pay your money and you've got to make a point of looking at it. Disregard [the relative cost] and if I had a choice I would go and see it on the big screen – it's a better effect."

Moreover, although it was the husband who was initially the keener on getting the video (not least so that he could tape his darts matches), it is his wife who is now its strongest supporter (in this case because of her particular use of the video to time-shift and repeat children's programmes when she's childminding). While the husband says that "if it went tomorrow I don't think I'd miss it", his wife, despite the expense of renting it, is anxious to keep it: "We got it before Christmas. I was scared to get it at first. I don't know why, he was always for it and I was always against it. I thought it was a waste of money, but since having it I wouldn't be without it."

Family 2

This couple are both in their forties, with a boy of eighteen and a girl of fifteen. Both husband and wife left school at fifteen. He is an unemployed painter and decorator. They live in a small, relatively modern and well-furnished council house. They have lived here for five years and have friends and relatives in the nearby streets. They have one colour television set, a video and one black and white set. The husband is a boating enthusiast and both are Ecology Party supporters.

The father in this family begins by guiltily describing himself and his family as "telemaniacs, I admit" in so far as they watch television every evening. However, he goes on to qualify the statement by noting that, of course, "If there is nothing on, we turn it off. We don't just watch it. It's mainly what we like to watch – we just watch it. If not, we just turn it off. We don't sort of stay there and watch it all the time."

Moreover, it soon becomes clear that, as in the case of a number of the other families, the husband watches television more than his wife, who claims that she "doesn't watch it that much". The family's basic viewing pattern is for the husband and wife and their daughter to view the main set in their living-room, while their teenage son watches separately on a black and white set in his bedroom. As his mother puts it, "He usually watches those horror films. They're in black and white anyway, so he's all right."

As a matter of routine the television may go on at 4.30pm when their daughter comes in from school, but generally it goes on at about 6.30pm, for *Crossroads*, when the mother has finished making tea, although they also remember one special occasion when the father watched something (a "lifeboat" programme – see below for his interest in this) at 5.30pm. After this point the television will normally be on most of the evening but they do "turn it off anyway, if company comes".

However, while the set is on, the different members of the family clearly attend to it in quite different ways. In terms of style of viewing there is a clear gender divide in this family, the man and his son preferring to watch attentively, in silence, and unable to understand how the wife and daughter can watch and talk at the same time.

Man: "We all stare a bit. We don't talk. They talk a bit."

Woman: "You keep saying ssh!"

Man: "I can't concentrate if there's anyone talking when I'm watching. But they can. They can watch and talk at the same time really."

Daughter: "Wondering what'll happen next week."

Woman: "I wonder if so-and-so is going to ..."

Man: "We just watch it – take it all in. If you talk, you miss the bit that's really worth watching. We listen to every bit of it and if you talk you miss something that's important. My attitude is, sort of, 'Go in the other room if you want to talk!'"

This difference also extends to the likelihood of talking to people about things they've seen on television. The man is unlikely to do this to any great extent: "I might mention it occasionally, but I really don't talk about it to anyone."

Conversely, his wife is very likely to talk to her sister about what she's watched, and their daughter is likely to spend time at school talking to her friends about *Dallas* and *Dynasty*, especially in discussions of the various characters' dress or skirt-lengths.

As is the case with many of the other families, the technology (the automatic control device and the video) is dominated by the father. They have two controls, one for the channel control and one for the video, and the daughter notes acidly that her father keeps "one on each side [of his chair]". He himself admits that he is a heavy user of the channel control and that he is often to be found "flicking about all the time, like . . . you know, instead of sometimes looking in the paper you just sort of go – you go flicking over at nights . . . just leave it on. That's when you're in that type of mood for doing it."

As the husband is the person who is likely to stay up latest to watch television (a common pattern among the unemployed men in my sample), he often gives way in the case of a conflict over channel choice: "Usually, I'll say 'Right, if we're going to watch either one or the other, tape mine and I'll watch it later on.'" This is felt to be only reasonable by all concerned. As his wife states, her husband will watch what he's taped earlier in the evening and "we go to bed and he stays up and watches it".

Here again it was the husband who was the prime mover in getting the video. As his wife says: "There was a serial which was – *Shogun* – and we got it for that, actually, 'cause you was working away at the time and we was thinking of buying one and when we knew that was coming on, 'cause they advertised it and it looked good, we said, 'Oh yes, we'll get it,' and my husband got it and we used to tape it each week for him."

During the period when they first got the machine, when they were renting a lot of video films, it was mainly the husband who would go to the shop and select the films (another common pattern among the families I interviewed). They primarily use the video for time-shifting broadcast programmes now, something which they do "near enough" every night. However, like many women, the wife found the video machine very hard to master, especially at first: "There's things I've wanted to watch and I didn't understand the box. She [their daughter] used to understand it more than us."

Like a number of the other teenagers in the sample, their daughter sometimes engages in socialised video watching with her friends, one of whom in particular "gets everyone from school and they watch the film and then have a discussion after it. She'll invite people round and say, 'I've got this film and I'm showing it at a certain time. Do you want to come?'"

The mother and her daughter, like most other women in my sample, are principally interested in soap opera. The mother's attitude to *Crossroads* is equivocal; she has watched it for years and still does, despite feeling that it is "not very good": "I keep saying it's

not very good, but I still watch it! I say, 'Oh, it's not as good as it used
to be, but I'm just going to see what's happening,' you know..."

Her daughter tends to be busy with her homework while
Crossroads is on and thus frequently misses it. However, she ensures
that she finishes her homework in time for *Coronation Street* which
she likes because she feels the characters are "more true to life". She
also rather likes *EastEnders*, but her mother is very critical of the
programme – because she thinks that it is not realistic and it certainly
does not provide her with an image of herself (as an "East Ender")
with which she can identify: "I don't think it's true to life, 'cause I
come from the East End, so I know what it's like. I don't know really.
They seem a bit aggressive and people must think everyone's like that.
But they're not – just they want to give that impression." This is a
theme to which she returns several times in the discussion: "I think
the *EastEnders* – it seems to me they always seem as if they're trying to
brainwash us, like I get that impression when I'm watching that
EastEnders as if they're sort of trying to make you – I don't know, I
can't explain it – trying to make you think a certain way. And you're
watching that day after day, you sort of start to – I don't know, it sort
of affects you a bit, like you start to accept the way they are for real.
They all talk aggressive to each other and always seem to be arguing. I
mean, you do argue, and there is aggressive people, but nearly all of
them on there are like that and it's not really true to life."

However, despite the woman's dislike of the programme, she
watches it with considerable interest, simply because it is about the
East End, where she grew up. As her husband puts it later: "You
usually like watching things about – like *EastEnders* – anything to do
with the East End, like. She'll watch it, you know. Any articles about
it ..."

Woman: "I s'pose so, yes... It's an interest, more than a
hobby... sometimes they have documentaries on the East End and
how it used to be."

However, some fictional representations of the area can win her
approval, certainly more than *EastEnders* currently does, as long as
they are "true to life": "There was a serial on, a good few years ago
now, about a docker from the East End. It was fiction but I liked it,
'cause it was all round that area, about this person and his family and
he got married and it just went on and on, but it was interesting...
and it was pretty true to life."

Like many of the women interviewed, the only form of news or
current affairs programming in which she has any interest is the local
news: "I like the one that's just after the main news, for about five
minutes [that is, *Thames News*]. I've got something about that – I
have to see it... Yes, it's only on for about five minutes. They tell you

all the news – not as much as the other one, though. But they seem to tell you more."

One interesting aspect of gender difference in relation to programme preferences emerges in the discussion of *That's Life*, which the female members of the family like but the man finds embarrassing except when it is dealing more formally with matters of social justice. His attitude is quite equivocal here; he likes the programme, but there is something about the personalised style of presentation (which his wife and daughter enjoy) that he finds problematic: "Sometimes on *That's Life* they tell you things that happen to people and it's interesting – like something that's happened to someone and it isn't right and they bring it out and they look into it and try to get it reversed. Sometimes it's very good when they do that." However, "I don't know. Some of the characters in it ... when she goes out interviewing people and they all act silly and all that, you know, that side of it ... I just don't like it, you know. It's not my cup of tea. It's a bit embarrassing, actually, watching it."

This gender difference is also linked to a misunderstanding which the husband has about why his wife and daughter used to watch *Blankety Blank* – which was precisely to do with the style of presentation rather than the "content" of the show: "I don't like that *Blankety Blank*. They love that. I can't stand it!"

Woman: "No we don't. We used to like it with Terry Wogan."

This gender difference in the "angle of interest" in television and its personalities also emerges in the discussion of the relative merits and "uses" of newspaper and *Radio Times* and *TV Times* material on television programming. The man's preference is strongly for the newspaper, because he finds it easier to use when planning his viewing choices. He says of *Radio Times* and *TV Times* (which they used to get), "Yeah, but funnily enough I never used to ... my wife used to look at that, but I always look in the paper."

Woman: "Yes, but you used to get mixed up and used to say you couldn't understand it. You used to say it's too much looking through, you know – with all the pages."

Man: "As I say, you've got your choice laid out, all on one page [in the newspaper]. It's either that or that ... it's clearer."

However, his wife's interest in the *Radio Times* and *TV Times* was not simply for programme information on which to base viewing choices, but for something else entirely: her interest in the people in the programmes: "*TV Times* was really just for ... if there's certain programmes on, they'll tell you about the actors and things like that."

The husband and son in this family conform directly to the classic pattern of "masculine" (that is to say, factual/documentary) viewing – in this case focusing on scientific and "nature programmes". The husband, moreover, is, like a number of other men in the sample, the only family member who consciously plans his viewing choices: "Yeah, we look in the papers. I usually mark 'em off, don't I? All the things like, 'cause if I don't mark 'em, sometimes I'll miss 'em. And all the nature programmes – I just mark all the things I want to watch. I look at it and say, "Oh yes, I'll watch that", and then I turn it off till the next programme comes on I want to watch. With me I like nature programmes and scientific ones. I know, James Burke, we was going to tape it tonight, but we forgot to put it on, didn't we? It doesn't matter, but that's a scientific programme. But we're all like that, aren't we? We only watch what we want to. We don't just watch it for the sake of it."

Whereas his wife and daughter tend to watch ITV, he finds that "BBC2's got a lot of good things". In this family it is certainly a case of "Like father, like son". In the son's words: "I like scientific things. Anything about mechanics. I like scientific, animal things, something about plants or nature or anything like that. But things like *Crossroads*, they don't interest me very much."

Or as his father puts it: "I can sort of tolerate *Coronation Street*, but *Brookside* is really boring." And he notes that if *Dynasty* or *Dallas* come on, "I'll go out of the room... go and do something."

Conversely, his wife cannot bear the "nature" programmes that her husband and son like so much, especially not "those with all the insects". Moreover, she is unable to understand how her husband can watch "things about hospitals, when they're doing all those operations".

Her husband's "instrumental" explanation is exactly parallel to his previous comments on what he likes and does not like about *That's Life*: "Yes, but it's interesting. Like you see them operating. I know it's a bit gruesome, but it's interesting like – you see how they do it and the skill they use and ..."

Both father and son do make some exceptions in their basic disregard for fictional programmes. In the father's case his taste in fiction is for traditionally masculine genres: "A lot of science fiction films I like. Some war films – there was one last night. *Apocalypse* or something – about Vietnam, you know – or maybe a few horror films." His son claims that he'll watch "anything, as long as it's a film... old films... with round cars [*sic*] and that, and good actors in. If there's good actors, it's worth watching." Beyond this, his only other fictional preference is for *Minder* – precisely because he finds it realistic: "It's the characters. I like the characters. They're pretty true to life and all, that *Minder*, you know – like the remarks they make. They sort of call the police, they call them the filfth. I've never understood that, but they all say it."

For his father it is *Only Fools and Horses* that is the fictional and comic favourite: "Brilliant, that is. It doesn't seem like a show when you're watching. It's just you're in it with them and they just...it's just natural... it's got a sort of magic about it. You can get into it and enjoy it. It's hard to describe really, how to define it... I think you identify with them a bit, sometimes, when you see, like, you – you sort of identify with them... it's understandable... Some comedy shows you think you can see that if they're trying to make you laugh, but in that programme it seems as if they're not trying, it's just happening, you know."

However, this comic interest is an exception. The man's basic interests are very coherent, running from his programme preferences ("nature programmes, *Fragile Earth*, *Survival*" through his leisure activities ("He's got a boat"; "Yes, boats... well, sailing boats. I'm a bit of a fanatic") and his magazine purchases ("I get a lot of boating magazines – *Yachting World* and *Boat Owner* and *Yachting Monthly*," his library usage ("Mainly books about boats and the sea") to his voting intentions (Ecology Party). And he stresses: "Oh yes, if there's anything on the telly about lifeboats – anything to do with boats – I always watch it or tape it, definitely, yes."

This family also provide an interesting insight into the various modes of parental control of their children's viewing – not simply in terms of "censorship" or prevention, but also in terms of the use of sarcasm and forms of indirect pressure. The mother is in part puzzled by her daughter's ability not to be bothered by horror films: "Well, horror films – she's not really scared. Sometimes I say, 'Oh, you can't watch that,' and she says, 'Oh, I want it to be more horrible! It's not frightening enough!'" The mother says, "We never stop them watching anything. We used to stop them watching horror films when they was a bit younger, but not so much now." However, the father remembers that: "When *Grange Hill* came on I was a bit 'iffy' about that... and she [his daughter] used to like it. We never used to stop her seeing it, but I didn't really like it and didn't like her looking at it. There again, like *Grange Hill*, the kids were a bit aggressive to each other and always seemed to be in a temper or something, you know. But I would never stop her, I don't see the point of it really."

At this point their daughter slightly alters this picture of total liberalism by remarking forcibly that although they never stopped her watching *Grange Hill*, her father did pressurise her about it in a way that she found quite uncomfortable. "No, you just used to come in and say, 'You're not watching that rubbish, are you?'"

Family 3

The husband in this family is in his mid-forties. His wife is thirty-five, and they have girls aged fourteen and six, and a boy of eleven. Both parents left school at fifteen. The husband is an ex-gardener and horseman who has been unemployed for some time. His wife works as a part-time doctor's receptionist. They live in a small council house and have lived there for seven years, with relatives living nearby. They have a home computer besides one colour television (with teletext), one black and white set and a video. The husband keeps budgies for a hobby. He is a Labour voter, his wife a Liberal voter. They haven't had a holiday in the last year.

This family is very much dominated in its viewing habits by the father, who describes himself as "addicted – it's like a dope to me". In this house the set is on "every night ... and most days as well. In the holidays it's on from breakfast time till the dot at night. I normally put it on at about 12.30pm for the news – and *The Sullivans*. It's on then till the dot comes up. At weekends it's on all day. Saturday it's on from the time she gets up, the little 'un, to the time I go to bed."

The distinction here is not between watching television or switching the set off: it is between watching television and turning the sound down but leaving the set on. As the man puts it, he will often watch "whatever follows on. If it's interesting, we watch it. If we're not interested, it's just on – I mean like Saturday afternoons you've got sport. More often than not I don't even look at it. It's just background noise, because I hate sport."

Even disliked material such as sport is "something to look at". The continuity of viewing (in its various modes) extends even to the interview situation itself: "I mean, I haven't turned it off now, even though you're here. It doesn't matter who comes in, the telly'll still be on. If they [the children] want to watch something we turn it up. Apart from that, it's on, but there's no sound. I'm watching it all the time I'm talking to you. I know it's very rude, but ... I still change it over – like I changed it over just now when we was talking – even when my friends come in. I know what programmes I want and I change it over to the programmes I want."

This man has the common masculine obsession with watching television in uninterrupted silence. He experiences some difficulty in doing this, because the other members of the family do not share his viewing tastes on the whole, and the children "muck about" while he's viewing. He responds by banishing them from the room. When asked if they talk while watching the television he replies, "No. We watch the telly. If there's any programme that I've got on – all quiet. If they're not quiet they'll be out."

His wife says that she is "not quite so bad" as him towards the children, but she goes on to explain that she has less reason to argue with them than her husband, in so far as her tastes and theirs coincide to a much greater extent: "I mean, most sort of programmes I think, as I said. I like *Dallas* and the children like *Dallas* – so they'll sit and watch it. So really it's not the same things, because the programmes I like they enjoy. I think he's worse than I am, definitely!"

Her husband readily confirms: "That's right... that's the difficulty. The programmes I want to listen to – they start playing about and fight. So they either go and watch the television upstairs or in the other room, or go to bed – or they've got to do the washing up, to do something, and leave me alone. I just want to sit here and watch the programme." He uses his power quite straightforwardly. As he says right at the beginning of the interview, "If I'm watching one programme and they [the children] want to watch another one, then I send them up there [to their room]. They watch what I want to watch – unless there's something special and they go upstairs and watch in the other room."

The husband also monopolises the symbol of power, the automatic channel control device. As his wife puts it: "I don't get much choice, because he sits with the thing beside him and that's it. I get annoyed because I can be watching a programme and he's flicking channels to see if a programme on the other side has finished, so he can record something. So the television's flicking all the time, or he's flicking the timer. I just say, 'For goodness' sake, leave it...'"

Interviewer: "So you don't use the machine, you don't – "

Woman: "I don't get the chance, I don't get near it!"

Conflict over programme choice is resolved quite simply in this situation – by the father's dictate. He doesn't like comedy programmes on the whole, whereas the rest of the family do. However, they are allowed to watch comedy programmes on the main set if it is one of the few comedians that the father likes. Otherwise "They don't get the chance to watch it, 'cause I don't let them have it on!"

Woman: "We don't normally have it on – unless, as he said, it's Freddie Starr or Jim Davidson, and then we can watch it." Interestingly, the very nature of this man's power causes some confusion at times – when he is unable, it seems, to distinguish between himself and the family as a whole.

Woman: "Well, we had an argument on Sunday. His mother turned up and he said, 'What about a cup of tea?' and I said, 'I'll get you one in a minute,' and he sat there watching, and he said, 'You've seen this.' I said, 'I haven't seen it.' He said, 'Well, I've seen it, so you must have done.' I said, 'I haven't.' So anyway I got up and made a cup of tea and come back and gave them a cup of tea, so I said, 'You could have made the tea. You've seen it. I haven't.' So he said, 'You must have seen it.' It worked out he'd recorded it and watched it when everybody'd gone to bed, that's why he'd thought I'd seen it too."

Man: "I thought I'd seen it in the evening, and I hadn't. In fact, I'd recorded it and watched it later."

This man is a dedicated homebody, for whom sitting at home watching television is preferable to just about any other activity: "We don't go out, so we've got to have the telly. I don't drink. This [television] is the only vice I've got – smoking and this. And it's not often you get me away from this... I don't want to go out."

This is something which his wife finds quite distressing. Her husband is reluctant to go out even when it's free and all arranged on his behalf: "What, once every six months! We went to see Freddie Starr Sunday night. The battle I had to get him there! Wimbledon Theatre. It was paid for by his mother. She bought the tickets for his birthday – it didn't cost us a penny. Some friends even came and picked us up in the car. I enjoyed it. He enjoys it once he gets there! Once he's there, he's all right! It's just the hassle of getting him going. You know, moving out of his chair sort of thing. Once he's there he's fine."

None the less, as far as her husband is concerned, "I'd sooner sit here. I'm far happier like this. As long as I've got something to watch on the telly. I would sooner have gone and bought seven films or ten films than I would have gone and seen Freddie Starr. I'd sooner sit here and watch... especially decent films."

The basis of the husband's preference for "staying in" is clarified later in the interview, when it becomes clear that the key factor is that in going out to a public place this man experiences a loss of the total power which he has established within the walls of his own home. Even if his examples (stretching his legs out, smoking, drinking tea) seem trivial, the point is that it is only in his own home that he can do precisely what he likes: "Plus you're in your own home. In the cinema you sit in your own little seat with no leg room and no smoking. Three hours with no smoking and I smoke heavy. I'd have to get up in the interval and go out, and you smoke about five in that five minutes and make yourself sick. Plus you can have a cup of tea and do what you like."

This man plans his viewing (and videotaping) with extreme care. At points he sounds almost like a classical utilitarian discussing the maximisation of his pleasure quotient, as he discusses the fine detail of his calculations as to what to watch, and what to tape, in what sequence: "And like evening times, I look through the paper and I've got all my programmes sorted out. I've got it on tonight on BBC because it's *Dallas* tonight and I do like *Dallas*, so... I don't like *Wogan*, but... We started to watch *EastEnders*, didn't we? And then they put *Emmerdale Farm* on, so we've gone for *Emmerdale Farm* 'cause I like that and we record *EastEnders* – so we don't have to miss out. I normally see it on a Sunday anyway. I got it all worked out to tape. I don't mark it [in the paper], but I register what's in there; like tonight, it's *Dallas*, then at 9pm it's *Widows* and then we've got *Brubaker* on until the news. So the tape's ready to go straight through. What's on at half seven? Oh, *This Is Your Life* and *Coronation Street*. *This Is Your Life* we have to record to watch *Dallas*. I think BBC is better to record, because it doesn't have the adverts. *This Is Your Life* we record because it's only on for half an hour, whereas *Dallas* is on for an hour, so you only use half an hour of tape.

"Yeah, Tuesday. If you're watching the other programme it means you're going to have to cut it off halfway through, and I don't bother, so I watch the news at nine o'clock ... Yes, 'cause there's a film on at 9pm on Tuesday, so what I do, I record the film so I can watch *Miami Vice* and then watch the film later."

The bottomless pit of this man's desire for programmes to watch cannot be entirely fulfilled by broadcast television, and before he became unemployed they were renting a video film practically every night as well as watching broadcast television. "If I could afford it, I'd have a film tonight, and every night." His interest in video films is supported through the relationship with his friend John. "Yes, I like to talk to John. That's my friend that comes on Saturday night, because he's a great video man. And the people opposite, they got their video just after us, and they'd never had a video and we'd never had one. And they got one – and often we used to talk about films then, didn't we? And if I had a film and I thought they'd be interested in it I'd watch it earlier on in the evening, then I'd drop it over there – and they used to do the same for me. But then that dropped out. I didn't bother any more. The people that come on Saturday night, he's got a collection of films, I think he's got fifty-six films, hasn't he? And when he went away on holiday last summer, he brought them over here. 'Look after this lot I've got here,' he said. 'Would you look after them?' He wanted me to look after them, you see he'd been broken into." This was clearly an experience close to Nirvana. "Yeah, we had fifty-six films that we watched in that fortnight. So, I mean, the cost was nothing. That was great."

As for programme preferences, what he likes is "police programmes, documentaries and prison films. I like prison films – anything to do with prisons." Beyond this, like a number of other men in the sample, he likes a range of documentary programmes: "I like all the African programmes, you know, they're going through Africa and interviewing all the Third World people. Yes, I like all their programmes, but my wife doesn't. Sometimes she'll watch it, but ..." What he doesn't like, on the whole, is comedy.

Man: "I don't ... I can't stand them."

Woman: "He's got no sense of humour!"

Man: "No, I haven't really! The only sort of people I like are Freddie Starr, Jim Davidson."

As for serials, it is *Hill Street Blues* ("I'm still watching that now, though most of it is repeats") and *Auf Wiedersehn Pet* ("That's a terrific programme") that are his particular favourites. Apart from these interests, as an ex-stableworker and a bird-fancier he has another set of viewing preferences as well: "About horses – yeah. Anything to do with horses – I mean I watch all the show jumping and programmes. Hickstead and the International Horse Show and things like that... No, but I noticed, I think it was last night on Channel Four – I'm not sure really, I think it was on Channel Four – there's a new series coming on about all different types of animals and pets. I only caught a glimpse of it last night and one series is about birds, and there's one about horses, so I'm looking out for them. They very rarely put anything on about birds. I mean, wild birds, yes, but not canaries that you can keep."

The wife has a much more "take it or leave it" attitude to television. She is much less interested in it than her husband (who says he "wouldn't know what to do with himself" without it). Thus she doesn't mind too much when he has things on which she doesn't like (or perhaps this is how she adapts to this situation), because, as her husband says, "She reads the paper or does knitting." As she puts it herself "That's it. I mean, I can do a crossword and forget it."

This attitude also means that she rarely bothers to video things for herself. As she says, she doesn't do this because, on the whole, she's happy with what she sees. "No, not very often, because I'm happy with what I see. I mean, lots of the films he records I don't even watch. He watches them after we've gone to bed – I go to bed about 11.30, 12pm, and he'll put it on." The exceptions are few and far between: "The only thing I did record was Elvis, his programme, which I kept. I kept it all the time... I would have kept the *Deerhunter* as well, but we weren't here at the time to record it. I've already seen it, but I would have liked to have kept it."

Her most enthusiastic comments are reserved for the period when she had their second television in the kitchen: "When he first brought it home I had it in the kitchen. I loved that – going out there and cooking dinner." In the main, she feels quite apologetic and even guilty about the organisation of their family life around the television. She admits that they eat all their meals in front of the television ("We've got all the bad habits") and goes on to pour scorn on the very programmes which she particularly enjoys, which she refers to as "Typical American trash really. I love it!" As she put it earlier on, what she likes is "All the American rubbish, really. I love

Australian films. I think they're really good, the Australian films."
She is as keen as most of the other women on soap operas: "Yeah,
Crossroads, I must see that every night - and *Emmerdale Farm*.
Dynasty, of course, and *Dallas*."

Apart from this type of material the wife also singles out, as being
of some interest, programming which has some relevance to her sense
of herself as a mother: "It's not that often you get one on, but it's just
- I mean, that *Boy David*, now that was terrific. I enjoyed that. The
boy who had no face - it was marvellous, what they done to him." She
also mentions programmes such as *Police Five* and programmes
which she feels are relevant to her own domestic responsibilities.
"The only sort of film I would say to them to watch is an educational
film, like if the police was to put one on about warning children about
strangers, then I would make sure they'd watch it...any sort of
warning films really. I would say, 'Just sit and watch that.' I mean
when Jimmy Saville used to have them on a Sunday, dangers in the
home, dangers on the road and all that, I used to say to them, 'Now
watch this,' because it's interesting, you can learn from them. And
that crime programme now - *Crime Watch* - that's a good
programme to watch because it gives you some idea of what to look
out for - what the kids should look out for as well. It's mainly
youngsters and old people that they set about, isn't it? But they don't
do those sort of films, do they? I mean, something like the warning
film for children by the police - I think they should show something
like that."

Like most of the women interviewed, it is local rather than
national news that engages her interest. "I watch the 1pm news and I
like *Thames News*. If I'm cooking dinner then I don't see it, but if I can
watch it, I'll watch the 6pm news and *Thames News* again on Friday,
with Michael Aspel."

In common with the mothers, she dislikes the *Young Ones*
intensely, although her daughter (like most of the teenagers) likes it
very much: "*The Young Ones* - I think it's a revolting programme.
The things they come out with in it. But you [that is, her daughter]
find it's funny, you think it's really funny don't you?"

The woman clearly talks regularly about the programmes and
videos she's watched with her friends at work: "*Boy David*, about that
boy, we discussed that. I had a set of films called *Those I Loved* which
was thoroughly discussed at work, and they're always saying to me,
'Have you had any good films lately?' *The Deerhunter* we discussed
when it was on television. But apart from that, *Dallas* and *Dynasty*,
obviously - we always discuss them. Well, just discussing them - 'Oh,
didn't she look stupid?' 'Have you seen...?' That sort of thing, you
know, sort of running it down."

Her tastes can also be seen to have a strong coherence across different media. "I'm looking forward to Richard Chamberlain (in *Wallenberg*). *Blockbusters* – I like the *Bestsellers*, any of the *Bestsellers* – they're very good. I like to listen to Simon Bates and his stories, and I used to love it on Radio One when they did all the old songs. As for books, I do like Harold Robbins and Catherine Cookson."

As already noted, the television technology is very much masculine-dominated in this family.

Man: "Most of the time it's me recording."

Woman: "It's you and Robert [their son] really, isn't it?"

Their son in fact uses the video quite a lot ("he brings films home, and he brings friends' films home") and it is his father who uses the teletext device most. Interestingly, the position is entirely reversed when we move from television and video to print. While his wife and children all read (and use their local library) quite extensively, the husband does not. As he puts it, somewhat bitterly, "I've never read a book in my life. I've not got the patience to read a book. I've got the patience to sit and watch the telly. I ain't got the patience to do anything else, like painting. I don't do anything really."

Family 5

The husband here is in his mid-fifties, his wife a little younger. They have two daughters (sixteen and twenty-four) still living with them. Both husband and wife left school at fourteen. He is an unemployed ex-ambulance man, who is now hoping to set up his own small business. His wife works full time as an occupational therapist in the local hospital. They are private tenants in a well-furnished house situated in the midst of a number of large council estates. They have lived here for seventeen years. They have one colour television set and a video. They took one holiday in the last year. Both husband and wife are Conservative voters and the husband is also a member of the Regimental Association Model Soldier Society. The man is a passionate supporter of all things British and traditional.

The wife in this family begins the interview by stating: "We are great television addicts. You name it, we watch it. I even watch in the afternoon – *Sons and Daughters*, *Gems* is my favourite in the afternoons, and the film on Monday sometimes. Some of the best programmes are during the day. I watch it at work quite a lot as well. They are always on in the ward. When you go in to get a patient you can get a quick look." As she explains, their television is on practically all the time in the evenings. "It doesn't often get turned off. It's mostly on during the evening. There's nearly always something one or another of us wants to watch. We play games – Scrabble and things like that. It's still on then." The only exception is if visitors come, a point which she repeats several times in the interview: "It's on all the time. Unless we've got anybody here of course. Then it goes off." We don't leave it on if there's anybody here…"If anyone comes, a guest or anything, we switch it off. One of the rules of the house."

Her husband has a very different attitude to television from his wife, and is at pains to present himself as discriminating in his viewing habits. He only watches during the day "if there is something to my taste". His programme tastes are very different and are a problem for his wife and daughters – especially now that he is unemployed. As one of the daughters says: "He likes opera and ballet and things like that – but now we all have to sit and watch it now he's at home." Conversely, their preferences are a problem to this man, who complains, "when it's on you've just got to watch it. I'm captive. This stuff I call rubbish [that is, what his wife and daughters like], I've got to watch it." He repeats the point later and explains that he deals with the problem by doing something else while the "rubbish" is on. "I'm not really an addict of TV. It's just that I'm captured. I get tired and sit down, so I'm a captive audience and I read the paper." Being outnumbered three to one as he is by his wife and daughters, although he disapproves of their programme choices (and although they do feel guilty about these "low-grade pleasures"), he simply has to put up with things much of the time, which he does rather resentfully.

Man: "I'm captive. The three of them gang up on me (though they often tape things for me). I do get annoyed sometimes. I come in here, and as far as I can see it's either a daft give-away prizes programme or a *Top of the Pops* programme."

In terms of viewing style the common pattern of gender difference recurs in this family. His wife explains that she and her daughters are not allowed to talk while watching. However, it seems that this rule is generally broken. As she says. "Oh, we do sometimes. Her and her boyfriend are like little rabbits, though we stop [talking] at all the best parts." This mode of viewing is simply incomprehensible to her husband. Not only does he disapprove of it, he can't understand how they manage it: "It really amazes me that this lot can talk and do things and still pick up on what's going on. To my mind, it's not very good if you can do that." To which his wife responds that it is a matter both of the type of programme they view, and of practice. She explains that the programmes she and her daughters like are "not really highbrow enough to get into it. With you and TV you really die. Us, because we have it on all the time, it's like second nature. We watch, and chat at the same time."

Given these strong conflicts over programme choice (and over viewing style) it is hardly surprising that the video plays a large part in maintaining social harmony, enabling them to avoid direct clashes. As the wife says, for them video "is an essential part of viewing...because you have a choice". She expands the point later: "In this house it's the ideal thing, because we keep such different times. I can't think how we managed before. I suppose we must have argued about it more. We still argue about everything now, because we're so different in what we like."

As the man is now unemployed, while his wife and daughters all go out to work, in cases of conflict over programmes he can usually be prevailed on to give way and tape his choice to watch it later ("because he doesn't have to get up in the morning"). However, although the video is used extensively within the family, it does not serve as the focus of any wider social occasion (for instance, other people being invited round to view something), "not unless we had a wedding [video] or something like that".

In terms of channel loyalties the common gender division whereby the wife prefers ITV and light entertainment and the husband prefers the BBC and factual programming is repeated here. However, it is BBC2 rather than BBC1 which this man prefers. "We are inclined to watch ITV more. He always puts on BBC2, no matter what's on," as his wife puts it.

Similarly the common gender positions in relation to news are repeated, with the wife rather self-conscious about her own (and her daughters') lack of interest in the news.

Man: "I tend to watch the 10pm news if it's on that side. They rush across to turn it off."

Woman: "Then someone will go and make the tea and leave him to it. What will people think when they read this? They'll think us morons!"

Like many of the other women interviewed it is only the local news which interests her: "ITVs best because that's London Weekend. It tells you what's going on in your area, so you are more interested."

Her husband's interest in the national news and current affairs programmes is a little spoiled, however, by his feeling that these areas of programming (especially on BBC) are so dominated by "left-wing bias". "I can't stand the BBC news because it's so...left-wing biased. ITV's getting a bit that way too. I love documentaries, but I do feel they are terribly biased. You see a lot of things about South Africa at the moment. They talk about violence, but why don't they go into these African countries that have dictators? Nobody knows about the violence and torture, the terrible violence...and Ethiopia..."

The man's view of children's television, and of *Grange Hill* in particular, is rather in the same vein: "I should think all parents want to send their kids to private school after watching [*Grange Hill*]. They are animals, those kids. It must be a bad influence."

His tastes are quite incomprehensible to his wife and daughters who remark disdainfully that it is "all the 'hi-brow' stuff, he likes – *Panorama*, *World in Action*, intellectual programmes". He adds that he also likes "those animal programmes, natural life series, opera. There isn't much on there that I watch." As he explains, he takes a very traditional view and is principally interested in television as an educational and informative medium, and as a mode of access to "art". "I tell you what I really do enjoy is the Open University programmes. I can't comprehend some of it, but some of the ones on art are so well produced. If you don't learn with those, you'll never learn." This concern with high art extends to other media as well. "I've got the boxed record sets. I always try to get the right orchestra with the right conductor and the right soloists and so on." However, "the only chance he gets to listen to all his classical music" is when the family are all out at work during the day or when he is on his own in the car.

Nowadays there is not really anyone whom he talks to about the programmes he watches on television, though previously "There was one chap [at work] who had the same taste as me, and we might have said to each other, 'Did you catch that programme?'" He is committed to a very distinct sense of minority/high culture and feels badly let down that Channel Four has not turned out to devote as much time to this type of material (especially classic "British heritage" material) as he and his friends had hoped. "I and my friends all looked forward to Channel Four, but now it's here it's no different from ITV. I thought it was going to cater for people like myself. More like BBC2. It's not lived up to it, and my friends agree. They could have used it for people like myself. There are so many good things that are missed – the younger generation will never see – *Henry V*, for example, classic films, *Wuthering Heights* – things like that."

This positive estimation of a "British tradition" also emerges negatively as anti-Americanism, and he identifies American programmes with the forms of television violence of which he disapproves (as an ex-ambulance man he feels he has seen enough real violence to have a special expertise on this point: "We could sell these [British series] abroad, rather than import the [American] rubbish we do . . . with the violence – the silly violence. I don't like children to see some of the violence. Being an ambulance man, I've seen violence. TV has a lot to answer for with children." He says that when he was an ambulance man he had "to take them to the hospital, I've got to pick them up from police stations and they have been imitating the characters on television. You see an old lady get cracked over the head on television and you don't see what happens afterwards."

The only form of lowbrow culture to which this man admits any inclination is horror films "really as relaxation" – this is what he gets from the video shop when he goes. But even then he quickly points out that he only rents these because the shop fails to supply the "good films" he'd really like to watch. His wife is slightly less convinced of this account of his motives:

Woman: "What have we had recently? Mostly horror films, aren't they. He likes horror films."

Man: "It's really something just to laugh at, relax, you know. Really and truly, though, the video shop doesn't carry a stock of anything that's sort of highbrow, or good films, you know."

Woman: "If you had a choice between a horror film and anything else you would still choose a horror film anyway."

Man: "Possibly!"

The man's main suggestion, in terms of new forms of programming which he'd like to see more of, is a "good hobby series" (his own hobby is collecting model soldiers): "That is something there could be more of – a good hobby series. Lots of people have gone back to the old crafts – like cane chair making. It could be done on a Sunday afternoon."

His wife and daughters are straightforward fans of soap opera, although his wife is mildly embarrassed at admitting it. "I like all the soap operas. You name it, we watch it. We watch them all. We watch *Brookside* on a Saturday, *EastEnders* on a Sunday. We sound real morons, don't we! We're hooked on *Emmerdale Farm* now. It's on at 7pm, so we can watch it. It used to be on about 5pm just when we got home from work and I'd be out in the kitchen doing tea while everyone was sat down watching it, and I'd be saying, 'What's happening, what's happening?'"

Daughter: "I like *Lace* and *Princess Daisy*, those bestsellers you can really get lost in. I really like *Falcon Crest* – I really think they ought to bring that back. I think it's better than *Dallas* and *Dynasty*. I like them, but not as much as *Falcon Crest*. *Dynasty* is our favourite, I think."

Her mother says simply, "*Crossroads, Coronation Street*. We watch all the soap operas. It's only because we haven't got much else to do."

At this point her husband suggests that he doesn't know "why they don't put all the soap operas together and make one big thing". At this his wife cannot help pointing out his incompetence as a viewer of soap operas (and presumably, therefore, the invalidity of his opinions): "The way you talk about them, you'd think they did. He gets all the names and characters mixed up."

Clearly the taste conflict between this couple is quite strong, and there are various forms of accommodation and negotiation of this conflict. On the one hand, his wife notes, "There's one thing we don't have on when he's here. We don't have the games programmes on, because he hates them. If we women are on our own here – I love it. I think they're lovely!" On the other hand, for serious pleasure, this woman prefers to schedule them for occasions when she's alone and can enjoy things fully, without her husband's disapproval spoiling her fun. "If I'm here alone, I try to get something a bit mushy and I sit here and have a cry, if I'm here on my own. It's not often, but I enjoy that."

Moreover these solitary pleasures are also very likely to provide the material for her social interactions when she goes to work, where talk about soap opera seems to be a fairly constant feature. "At work we constantly talk about *Dallas* and *Dynasty*. We run them down, pick out who we like and who we don't like. What we think should happen next. General chit-chat. I work with quite a few girls, so we have a good old chat." Discussions are along the lines of "who is good looking and who do you fancy, and if they should be paired up with each other".

Interestingly, she is very aware of the way in which class differences emerge at work in these discussions – as between the occupational therapists and the domestics, and is well aware of her own "midway" position between the two groups as an Occupational Therapist (but less qualified and older than the rest) who has in many ways, more in common with the domestics. "At work there's OTs and domestics. There's a wide range of tastes. I'm the cheap, common one amongst the lot of them. They are all very highbrow, university types apart from the domestics. The OTs are definitely different from the domestics and I'm sort of a bit in between really. I'm a lot older. They're all quite young, so we do have different tastes, but we do have some really interesting discussion about TV. We haven't got much else in common, so we talk a lot about TV."

Moreover, while her husband's work experience as an ambulance man makes him hyper-critical of hospital programmes' lack of realism, this does not seem to be a problem to her or her daughters, although they all work in hospitals.

Woman: "You don't like hospital programmes, do you? Doctors series he can't stand. He sits and picks faults all the time. Saying things like 'If they did that, he'd be dead by now.'"

Daughter: "We love it, think it's great – *Angels*, *Young Doctors*, that sort of thing."

The wife identifies strongly with certain portrayals of the white working class on television – particularly *Only Fools and Horses*, which matches with her own perception of the East End. "What was our favourite one? Dell Boy in *Only Fools and Horses*. He's a great character, that bloke. Because we go to the East End quite a lot. We go to the market – we go over there most Saturdays. Seeing Dell Boy, it's like meeting up with characters you meet when you go over there." By this same criterion she also liked *Fox* and *Out*, but it is also what makes *EastEnders* ring false to her: "*EastEnders* is nothing like it is in real life – because we know about the East End. I like that kind of people anyway. That's why I like *Fox* – that was done in the East End, and *Out*. I thought *Fox* was brilliant – they should bring that back." She also likes period drama. "*When the Boat Comes In* was brilliant. We watched that regularly – especially the period things. I mean, the clothes and things are so authentic. BBC are brilliant with clothes and sets." Basically, she likes watching fiction on television. Indeed, as she says, "My hobby must be television. I can relax and forget things and problems."

Family 6

This couple are both aged forty-four, with two sons (twenty and seventeen) and two daughters (sixteen and thirteen) all living in their small flat on a large council estate. Both husband and wife left school at sixteen. He is an unemployed ex-building worker, she is a full-time housewife. They have lived in the same flat for thirteen years, close to a number of their relatives. They have not had a holiday in the last year. They have one colour television set and one black and white, a video and a home computer. Their home, though cramped, is comfortably furnished. Both husband and wife are Labour voters. This man has a wide range of interests (from snooker and racing to yoga, mysticism and poetry) which he has developed while being unemployed (he spends part of each day in the local library).

The television is almost constantly on in this house. As the wife says, "When the children are home, it's twenty-four hours a day. They get up and switch on straight away and watch *TV-am* till they go to work. You can walk into this house at 7am and there's three of them sitting in front of the fire watching *TV-am* – and nobody'll move."

The husband is unemployed and often watches television during the afternoon. "I watch my racing and me pool in the afternoons. The kids put it on when they come home from school – 3.30 till 11.30pm." And unemployment means that there is little money for "going out". "We don't go out a lot, so we stay in and watch the TV."

In this family the two sons have their own television set in their room upstairs. The basic viewing pattern is that the girls primarily watch the main television in the living-room with their parents, and the boys tend to view separately on their own set.

In terms of viewing style, while both the husband and wife claim to prefer to view attentively and in silence, they both admit in a wryly humorous way that this just does not happen (except when they each tape things to view on their own). Television viewing here is very much a social activity which takes place amidst ongoing conversation.

Woman: "I like to sit down in peace and quiet and watch something."

Man: "But she's the worst!"

Woman: "You can't hear anything 'cause they're all jabbering. So I think, Leave 'em to it – we all do it, everyone's talking."

Man: "Everybody's talking one after the other. It's like a madhouse, this is. They all talk about what they want to happen. And I was saying, 'Be quiet, how can we follow the story?' And someone else starts. Then the boy comes in and it's 'What's happened so far?' and I say, 'I don't know,' and they all go up the wall. We sit down watching *EastEnders* – and then they all start shouting!"

In terms of channel preference this couple's tastes are fairly well matched, in so far as they stick closely to the two main channels, and ignore BBC2 and Channel Four on the whole.

Woman: "What we don't watch a lot is BBC2 and Channel Four. We hardly ever watch BBC2. You only get these black and white films – it's rare you get anything decent on there."

There seems to be a relatively more even distribution of power in this family than in many others, with the husband less dominant in terms of imposing his own preferences, although he does remark at one point that while his wife "likes her *Dynasty*, she won't be watching it this weekend because I'll be watching pool!" And his wife, when asked later whether she ever attempts to control what her children watch, replies categorically (though not without a certain humour) "Me? I've never controlled anything!"

In terms of programme genre preferences this couple inhabit the classic form of gender stereotyping with the wife interested in fictional programming and the husband in factual programmes. When asked initially about their programme preferences, the husband mentions *Weekend World* as one of his favourites and the wife refers to the "Sunday film".

Woman: "I watch my film, Sunday afternoon, after I've done all the dinner and cleared up. I like my *Blockbusters*."

They expand on these preferences later in the interview in terms of what "type of stuff" they're each interested in.

Man: "I like all documentaries – the *London Programme*, *World in Action*. I like watching stuff like that – *Panorama*, *Weekend World*. I can watch fiction, but I'm not a great lover of it."

Woman: "He don't like a lot of serials."

Man: "It's not my type of stuff. I do like the news, current affairs, all that type of stuff."

Woman: "Me and the girls love our serials. We have them all weighed out. Like Sunday afternoons we get everything done, the ironing, everything up to date, and usually you'll hear the girls saying, 'Mum, you know what's on tonight – *Dallas*, and we'll get everything done by then."

As for news programming, the contrast could hardly be clearer. Whereas the husband claims to watch the news several times each night his wife (and his daughters: 'No, we're not into that') have little or no interest in news programmes.

Man: "I watch the news all the time. I like the news, that type of stuff – current affairs and all that.'

Woman: "I don't like it so much."

Man: "I watch the news every time, 5.40pm, 6pm, 9pm, 10pm I try to watch."

Woman: "I just watch the main news. So I know what's going on. Once is enough – then I'm not interested in it."

These basic gender preferences carry over into their other leisure interests – for instance, in terms of which types of books they read. Thus the wife (and her daughters) prefer exactly the same type of material in book form as they do on television.

Woman: "The girls do love stories. They like them – sit and read in their beds. I read the girls' love books – 'cause they like the same sort of thing that I do, so they get little sad, weepy stories or love stories, and they'll sit and read them."

What is most striking in the husband's comments on his reading habits is not just the way in which these are parallel to his viewing preferences, but the way in which he understands the terms "good" and "fictional" to be incompatible. "I use the library quite a bit. I mostly read mythology and ancient history – that's what I'm into. I didn't realise the library was so good. I thought it was all just fiction." This way of thinking also forms his attitude to television in general, but particularly his disapproval of the way in which "people" (he seems, in fact, to mean women particularly, but would probably feel the same about men who only watched fictional television) "get lost" in fictional programmes.

Man: "People [that is to say, women] get lost in TV. They fantasise in TV. It's taken over our lives." As far as he is concerned, this retreat into the "little world" (that is, the feminine/domestic world) of fictional television is reprehensible. It is, in his view, an abrogation of one's civic responsibilities as an adult, which involve at least being informed about the real state of the world. "People today are coming into their front rooms, they shut their front door and that's it. They identify with that little world on the box."

This is all quite at odds with his wife's view of the matter, which is much more focused on the practical benefits of staying in and watching the television or video when you are not well enough off to do much else. "To me, I think it's better, 'cause if you can't afford to go out, you'd only get yourself in debt. So you come home, watch your telly, and if you've got a video you can put a film on."

Her husband in fact agrees strongly about the benefits of the video. As he puts it: "It's cheaper to run a video really – because you can sit indoors and have a drink and you don't have to go running around anywhere and you just sit down and relax and watch a film. It's even better than actually going out, you know."

Nonetheless, he does feel that there is a problem about watching exclusively fictional television in the way in which his wife does. He later goes on to say that her attitude will lead to television "taking over" her life. As far as she is concerned, she is happy for this to happen – as long as she is deriving her own pleasures from the experience. She simply doesn't make the same sharp distinction which he makes between (fictional) television and real life.

Woman: "To me, I think telly's real life."

Man: "That's what I'm saying, telly's taken over your life."

Woman: "Well, I don't mind it taking over my life. It keeps me happy."

Given their quite different tastes, one way in which they resolve their potential difficulties is simply by getting out of each other's way when the other party's favourite type of material is on, or by time-shifting their favourite programmes to a time when their partner is absent, so that they can then more enjoy their "favourites".

Thus, the wife explains that whenever the sport comes on "If there's anything like that on I usually go and do the ironing or else do something else – 'cause that don't interest me. I get all fidgety, so I'm better off out."

Her husband particularly enjoys viewing his favourite things late at night when everyone else is out of the way. "I like, on Saturday nights, the old films – and all the kids are upstairs in bed. I listen to country music as well all by myself in peace and quiet." Similarly, he is prepared to time-shift favoured material which no one else likes precisely so that he can then enjoy it more fully at a later point, when everyone else is out. "I like my *Weekend World* and the *Survival* progs. Sometimes I video them and watch them when they're not here."

His wife does exactly the same with her favourite material – her "weepies", of which her husband so disapproves: "If I like a good film on there, I'll tape it and keep it, especially if it's a weepy! I'll sit there and keep it for ages. Especially in the afternoon, if there's no one here at all, if I'm tired, I'll put that on – especially in the winter – and it's nice then, 'cause you sit there and there's no one around."

She and her daughters also go to the length of compiling videos of serialised best-sellers to watch in the same way, "of an afternoon", when she's free of domestic responsibilities and her husband is out. "We get those *Bestsellers* and put them together, so you get the whole series together, which is better than seeing a little bit at a time. Especially if it's late at night, you're so tired. It's nice to watch the whole film together, and you don't forget what's happened. We try and keep them so, of an afternoon, if you haven't got a lot to do, you can sit and watch it."

Clearly, their video plays a large part in allowing each of them to transform the schedule into a pattern whereby they can replace disliked material (in her case "news") with more of the programme types in which they are interested.

Woman: "We watch *Widows* and then play that another two or three times. It's the same with *Minder*. We get *Minder*, tape it, and when the news comes on we play it again."

The woman explains that her teenage daughters have a strong preference, within the realm of fictional material, for that which is "down to earth", a preference which, as she explains in her comments on *Widows* and *Fame*, she shares herself: "The girls love *Brookside*. Like *EastEnders*, it's down to earth. Like, in *Brookside*, there's kids out of work and things like which is going on today and they swear – because you do, everyone swears, and the kids have rows with their parents, which most kids do. And they get up to mischief, which most kids do. That's what the kids like. It's no good watching a false thing on there, but they like *Widows* – because that is more or less down to earth as well. Things like that. It's like *Fame* – when it was on in the beginning it was a bit down to earth, but now it's gone right over the top, so the kids never watch it."

Her daughters themselves explain that the programmes they like are "*Dallas, Dynasty, Brookside, Coronation Street* – because they are about people and their problems". In fact it transpires that the younger girl prefers *Dallas*, and it is the older one who shares her mother's preference for the "down to earth". She prefers *Brookside* "Because it's about neighbourhood problems...and *Dallas* is just false. It's a neighbourhood thing, isn't it? They go to each other with their problems and that. It's good."

This strong sense of connection between their concrete experience of neighbourhood and domestic life and their programme preferences is well expressed in their mother's comments on the way in which she talks about the fictional series which she watches with her women friends. "I go around my mate's and she'll say, 'Did you watch *Coronation Street* last night? What about so and so?' And we'll sit there discussing it. I think most women and most young girls do. We always sit down, and it's 'Do you think she's right last night, what she's done?' 'I wouldn't have done that', 'Wasn't she a cow to him?' 'Do you reckon he'll get...', 'I wonder what he's going to do?' Then we sort of fantasise between us, then when I see her next day she'll say, 'You were right, love,' or 'See, I told you so.'"

This is no naive failure on her part to distinguish between fiction and "real life". On the contrary, her very interest in this type of fiction centres on its close connection with her own experience of domestic life and relationships, and her discussions about the programmes with her friends are clearly charged with a whole range of moral and social calculations about the rightness (or wrongness) of particular types of action and about their probable consequences – calculations which depend precisely on the development of particular feminine forms of cultural competence. "It's like real life to me, because programmes like that are down to earth and it does happen. You think in your own mind what you would think of it if it happened to you. Then you see what your mate thinks. I think that's why most women watch that kind of thing. Well, all my friends do."

Just in case anyone (male) should be about to sneer at her viewing preferences, she ends by adding, in a slightly acid tone, "I mean, I don't sit and watch cowboys."

Turning to the way in which they use their video, it is clear that here again the technology "belongs" to the boys. As the husband (who, being unemployed, also stays up late to watch things he has videoed during the evening when the others are viewing) puts it: "I use it most – me and the boys more than anything, mostly to tape the racing, pool, programmes we can't watch when they [the women] are watching."

His wife's relationship to the video has, in fact, to be mediated through her daughters. As she explains, it is quite simply that her education entirely failed to provide her with any sense of understanding and confidence in relation to technology and therefore she never operates the video herself. "When I was at school we had nothing like that [computers, etc.]. I suppose that's why I won't touch it, in case I break it. I'd probably touch the wrong key and they'd go up the wall." Like a number of the other women, if she wants something taped she gets her daughters (who have used computers and videos in school) to do it for her: "Usually, as he [her son] goes out he'll leave a little list with the girls. Not with me, because I wouldn't do it – 'cause I do not understand it. Well, I haven't got the patience and I'll say to the girls, 'Tape that for me,' but otherwise I don't, very rarely, tape it. No, I leave them to tape it, because, well, I'm all fingers and thumbs."

For her daughters, like a number of the other teenagers in the sample, video plays a large part in the organisation of their social lives. As their father comments: "The kids have their little mates in – Saturday, if I'm not here, they all have their mates in. Either they have their friends round here, or they tape a film and take it to their mate's house and watch it down there when their mum's out. As long as the mum and dad's not there they are happy."

What is striking in their mother's comments is the amount of support she clearly gives to this kind of activity – very understandably, as it means that she and other mothers do not have to worry so much about where their children are, if they are known to be simply watching videos at a friend's house. "Because if it's late nights, they can bring their mates in – if they've got a film. And they've only got to go along the road. And I know they're all in . Their mums know where they are and they haven't got to worry. I like it because I know all the kids are in."

(ii) C₂ families

Family 7

This couple are both in their late forties with two daughters of nine and ten. Both husband and wife left school at fourteen. He is a service engineer; she is a part-time cleaner/kitchen helper in a local school. They own their small house and have lived there for twenty-eight years (moving there from the other end of the street). They have known each other since childhood and have a number of friends and relatives living in adjacent streets. They have one colour television, two black and white sets and a video, and have been away on a number of "weekend holidays" during the last year. The wife is a church-goer and is also treasurer of the Catholic school where she works. They are both Labour voters.

Viewing in this family is simply what happens in the evening, every evening, in a fairly automatic way. As they say, "It automatically goes on, really." They have three different televisions and "They're all often all on – every night from about 7 p.m."

One set is the wife's and is in the kitchen. "One set is on for when I'm in the kitchen – like at breakfast, or when we're eating dinner. It just goes on like the wireless used to go on years ago." Clearly, she finds viewing while cooking particularly enjoyable. "I watch in the kitchen. I find it relaxing."

The main function of their multiple sets is not so that they can watch different programmes at the same time, but rather so that different family members can watch (probably the same programme) in different places. "The kids have a TV in their room. They watch at bedtime from 8 p.m. and we watch down here, and if the wife is ironing she watches in the kitchen. Occasionally they're all on different programmes, but usually the same."

Watching television, as a category of activity, is clearly something that is done on the whole (certainly as far as the wife is concerned) as a background activity while also doing something else. As she says: "We don't sit, like..." Indeed, when first asked about watching television, her query "Do you mean sitting down?" immediately makes it clear that sitting down and watching attentively is a limited sub-category of the overall activity, as far as she is concerned.

The power structure in this family is by no means as obvious as in many of the others, as the husband is much less domineering in relation to programme choice conflicts, which tend to be resolved in favour of the children's preferences as long as they are still up. "We've never argued, like some families do. Bill's pretty easy really. He says if they [their children] want to watch it, let them, because you like reading, don't you?"

Man: "I don't really read books. I might read magazines – plumbing and heating, that sort of thing."

However, as in a number of other families, the overall pattern of gender relations is repeated in terms of both style of viewing and programme preferences. In the first case it is only the man who plans his viewing – checking the schedules in the paper: "Normally I look through the paper – 'cause you [his wife] tend to just put on ITV, but sometimes there is something good on the other channels, so I make a note. Things like films and sport."

As a shift worker, for whom video is a great boon, this also involves forward planning in relation to programmes which he wants his wife to tape for him. "I do a lot of shift work, so it's pleasant to have them recorded. I might read in the paper what programmes are on and say to her, 'Will you tape it for me?'"

The husband's programme preferences are characteristically masculine: "The news – I always watch the ten o'clock news, I like documentaries – sort of abroad, like Africa. Nature ones, too, they're quite good. Plus I like *Sweeney* – things with police in them." And he has no interest in soap opera: "I never watched *Coronation Street*, I don't think."

Woman: "He never got into it, this is it."

Equally predictably, his wife's prime interest is in fiction, and in realist soap opera in particular. "The children watch, and like, *Brookside*. It's *EastEnders* I like. It's like everyday life. That's what I like. Plus *Widows*, that's very exciting."

They say that they never discuss television programmes at home but they each do so at work, where the gender determination of which programme types they claim to discuss is equally clear.

Man: "I think we do at work. Talk about sport mainly."

Woman: "At work, yes, mostly series – like we've all been discussing *Widows*."

Clearly, statements such as these demonstrate the influence of sex-role stereotyping in daily life (and in this case working life) as much as they demonstrate their influence on viewing preferences (that is to say, these are statements about the gender *personas* each party adopts at work and the determinations these roles exercise as to what can be talked about), as well as simply being statements about what each party is interested in watching. The point is precisely that viewing behaviour cannot be understood in isolation from this wider pattern, and outside of its interconnections with these ongoing social roles.

Video has clearly affected their family life. They are conscious that: "It gives you the freedom to watch things when you want to really – the freedom to watch telly when I like." This is of particular significance for the wife, who derives great pleasure from watching her favourite programmes at times when her husband and children are out of the way, so that she can, for once, just concentrate on enjoying the programme without also having one eye (or hand) on her domestic responsibilities. "If Bill's taped something for me, I usually watch it early in the morning – about 6am. I'm always up early, so I come down and watch it very early about 6 to 6.30am Sunday morning. Now I've sat for an hour this afternoon and watched *Widows*. I like to catch up when no one's here – so I can catch up on what I've lost."

But this also bears on her enjoyment of breakfast television. Again, drawing on the argument developed elsewhere in this report concerning the need for the combination of programme preference plus time availability as the critical "formula" in understanding viewing behaviour, we can see these two factors clearly working in combination in the wife's account of her pleasure in watching a programme type she likes (chat shows) at a time which suits her well (early in the morning, before her domestic responsibilities have become pressing).

Interviewer: "Do you like chat shows?"

Woman: "Yes, that's why I like breakfast TV. I like them ones – particularly when I get up specially early on Saturday am to watch that on my own. I love Saturday morning breakfast TV. I'm on my own, because no one gets up till late. I come down and really enjoy that programme."

Family 10

This couple are both in their mid-twenties, with daughters aged three and six months. The husband left school at sixteen, his wife at seventeen. He works as a postman and is heavily involved in union activity at work. She looks after their two children full-time. They live in a maisonette on a large modern council estate. They have lived here for two years and previously lived only 200 yards away. They have relatives nearby, and the man has lived in this area since childhood. They have two colour televisions (one with teletext), two black and white sets and a video (as they can't go out much, because of their young children, they regard their expenditure on these forms of home entertainment as "money well spent"). They have taken three short holidays in their caravan during the last year. The husband is a member of the local Conservative Club (it has the cheapest beer) but is a staunch Labour Party supporter and was militantly involved in the anti-privatisation campaign in the Post Office. The wife is also a Labour voter, but would prefer to vote for Friends of the Earth if she "thought it would do any good".

This couple watch a lot of television. Indeed the wife describes their television as a "constant companion". They are very "interested" and critical viewers, who quite self-consciously use television in a very active way – as a stimulus for their own conversation and "debates".

The wife's daytime routine is clearly co-extensive with the television schedule: "Well, the baby wakes me up at 6.45 a.m. and the television goes on and we are up until about 11 p.m. and it's still on. My other one is three now and has started going to playschool in the morning, so that's about the only time it's turned off. It's a constant companion, our television – especially weekends. The three of us sit here, and it's on. She [the toddler] even does exercises with Lizzie on *TV-am*."

The couple are quite aware that it is their situation as parents of young children that ties them to the house and thus they turn to the television and video rather than to the pub and the cinema for their entertainment. Their attitude is to make the most of this situation and to make the best of what television has to offer.

"We have got three [televisions]. We have got one downstairs and one at my mother's. My mother-in-law has got the black and white portable and we have got the colour television in the bedroom. We could watch television anywhere. We like telly. I have got another telly – one of these four-inch radio and alarm ones – so really we have four sets. We used to go to the pictures and the pub. Now it's our entertainment – the telly and the video. We hire the whole package – the video, TV and cabinet for £27 per month. To me that's £27 well spent."

This couple have a quite distinctive attitude to the use of television for conversational stimulation, even to the extent of deciding to watch programmes featuring people who they dislike precisely in order to stimulate their own "debates".

Woman: "We like debates. We have lively debates. We like *Question Time*. Not all the time. We are watching now because Robin Day is on. I can't stand him. He winds me up something terrible. He's so incredibly ignorant and right wing."

At one level this couple display fairly stereotyped sex-role preferences in terms of programme types. The man is a great fan of "classic" gangster movies. "Mind you, Humphrey Bogart and Edward G. Robinson ... If they are going to show an old film they ought to make it a gangster film." Equally stereotypically his wife is a "weepie" fan: "I would want to watch the sloppy films. He hates it. We just watched a film recently, in the afternoon. The school bus is hit by a train and she lost her legs. I mean I don't mind watching them. I know they are going to end up happy."

Man: "There is too much tragedy in life to watch that."

Woman: "But when you have never experienced anything like that you like to sit and watch knowing that it is going to end up happy. I don't mind those sort of things. He won't watch."

In connection with this type of material they simply cannot understand each other's reactions, as is made clear in this discussion of *Sophie's Choice*.

Woman: "He saw *Sophie's Choice*, which I thought was a woman's film, and he came home. I mean I cry at Lassie on the telly, and he said to me, 'Don't watch it.'"

Man: "I was at work, and there was twenty other blokes in the room, and I sat there and the tears were rolling down my face. She sat there and watched it and nothing happened!"

There are some areas where their preferences and responses diverge quite sharply – partly because of the husband's stronger and more sharply articulated sense of class (and indeed of class hatred!).

Woman: "I also like the horse trials – which he doesn't like."

Man: "I can't stand anything to do with horses. Don't forget I have to work in South Kensington all day long. I can't watch horses without thinking of the ponces I deliver to all day long. That to me is an upper-class play thing. I've got nothing against horses. It's the people."

However, on the whole, their tastes are much less divergent than those of most of the couples interviewed in my sample, principally because of the way in which the wife's proto-feminism is also articulated as a dislike of most soap opera, which distances her from the other "mums" she mixes with but brings her tastes closer to those of her husband. As the husband puts it: "We are lucky really. We are pretty tuned in together. It is very rarely that I have to go downstairs and watch the telly. We are pretty tuned in to watching the same type of programme."

His wife explains that neither of them like most soap opera, and it becomes clear that the central criterion which they share is that of realism – in terms of which much soap opera falls completely short, as far as they are concerned.

Woman: "He hates soap operas. Mind you, I'm the same. Some of them are watchable, but I mean . . . *EastEnders*, for example. Just take *EastEnders*, which is the most modern. I mean, that is about as realistic as, I don't know, me flying to the moon."

Man: "Oh yeah, but it's better than *Dallas*. I mean at least they are scraping a living. I mean everybody is earning at least two thousand dollars a week in *Dallas*!"

As the husband later explains, they both have a very strong sense of a London working-class identity, and for that reason they particularly like things like *Fox*, or the *Sweeney* (and indeed *South of Watford*, because of its particular sense of humour), which are set in contexts with which they can identify. "We like all those, and *Minder* because you can relate to them, you sort of know them and you know the area. If you go down the Castle you can meet them. If you live in London, you know them. But, then again, *EastEnders* is naff, it is not real. When I was a kid I used to live down World's End, when it was the world's end!"

This man is very interested in news and current affairs – and indeed in the whole range of "factual" programming, which he, like many of the other men in the sample, singles out as his key preferences. "I must admit I prefer more factual TV. I enjoy some of the *TV Eye*. We've just watched the *Trojan War* – that was brilliant. I enjoy series like that – like *Life on Earth*, wildlife programmes, and *World in Action*." This same criterion also informs his viewing preferences within the realm of fictional programmes, where it is things which he sees as basically realistic which he is interested in, precisely because it is based on fact. "I watched that [*Wallenberg*] because they can't change it too much. They can put bits in, but they can't change the story – you know the undertones are factual. I am interested in the Second World War – it was my subject when I took my O-levels. History – I really love history. After I left school, it is something I have really carried on. Even now we buy factual books. I do enjoy watching factual programmes. I think I would much rather watch a factual programme."

The same criterion also inflects his preferences within the realm of news programming, where he prefers that which provides more "depth". "I like current events on TV. We always watch the news. We watch the seven till eight news on Channel Four. Most people don't bother watching. At the moment that is the best news programme – and *Newsnight* on BBC2 – because it goes more in depth. When you watch the six o'clock news they skim over the surface, but if you really want to know, then it's either got to be *Newsnight*, if you are up late enough, or Channel Four."

This man could almost be quoting from C. Wright Mills as he explains that as a "working-class man", he likes to know "what is happening to me personally". This statement indicates precisely an attempt to develop an understanding of the broad political and economic context of his "personal" life: "I like to know about things; because, basically, I'm a working-class man and I like to know what is happening. I like to know what is happening to me personally." It is in this context that his particularly enthusiastic response to the *Boys from the Blackstuff* is best understood – as providing precisely that sense of a connection between personal experience and the broader societal dynamics which construct that experience. "The best play I have ever seen was *Boys from the Blackstuff* – that was brilliant. What I found was an affiliation. I found it funny, yet very sad. It makes you laugh and it makes you cry. When he went off his head, to me you can't get any lower – that was sad. It is factual now, when you think about it. It is a portrayal of the eighties man. I definitely find an affiliation with it. Everybody [at work] watched that but they don't understand it, a lot of them, I don't think. A lot of them watched it as a play, but it was a lot deeper. Even if you take it at face value, as a series of plays, it was very clever, very funny, but the underlying tones, it was very sad."

As noted earlier, the key factor in this family is the wife's alienation from the soap opera programming which most of the women in my sample prefer. This is the reason why this couple's viewing preferences are more compatible (and less sharply distinguished by gender) than most of the other couples interviewed. The woman here is quite self-conscious about the fact that when she "grew up" she stopped being interested in soap opera.

Woman: "It used to be before we were married. I mean I never went out. If *Dallas* was on I never went out. But since I've had the children it has changed, I mean I don't watch any of the soap operas at all. I don't watch *Dynasty*, I don't watch *Dallas*. I'm not interested in them now." As she notes, her alienation from this type of programming is a problem, in so far as it distances her from the other mums on her estate and makes talking to them more difficult. "Some of the other mothers I know at playschool watch *Dallas* and *Dynasty* and all that. They can't understand why I don't watch *Crossroads*. I mean, my mother-in-law is the only other person I can talk to. Even my own mum likes *Dallas* and all of them."

She gives a very perceptive account of the way in which most of the women she knows construct their conversations, and their relationships, on the basis of two areas of experience – child-care and soap opera – one of which she does not share. "Before I had either of the children I used to know a lot of people. And then all of a sudden you have children and you can't talk about anything else but them. And ninety-nine per cent of the women I know stay at home to look after their kids, so the only other thing you have to talk about is your housework or the telly – because you don't go anywhere, you don't do anything, and that is what is happening. They are talking about what the child did the night before or they are talking about the telly, simply because they don't do anything else, and a lot of them just watch the soap operas."

The other side of the coin is that she is also isolated among her women friends by her own enthusiams – for programmes such as *The Young Ones*, which her friends don't watch. "We were watching *The*

Young Ones the other night. Oh, we did laugh. You see none of the mums watch that. It's too intellectual for them. Now that has me in stitches, where they are locking him in the fridge and he falls out, and you see, to them, it's lost. It does not mean a thing. It must be on Monday night, because I went out on Tuesday, and I was still laughing about it, and I asked if they had seen it and they all asked, 'What is the *Young Ones?*' You can't explain it. Even though I'm a mum, I feel out of it because they don't watch what I do. They watch *Crossroads* and *EastEnders, Gems, The Practice.*"

She is also aware that there is quite a long thread of this kind of isolation in her experience of enthusiasm for television programmes which others in her social environment do not share. "There was only one thing I ever watched when I really did laugh so much I thought I'd die. It was a BBC2 play. All I remember was this girl's party, *Abigail's Party* [a Mike Leigh play] and the bloke had a heart attack on the floor and before that there was the bird with the glasses. He said to her, 'Do you want to dance?' and she got up to do the slow dance and he was standing there giving it all this, and we were all in fits. It was repeated on BBC1. I was still living at home, that's how long ago it was. I was in fits and yet nobody else watched it."

She is fundamentally isolated among the women she mixes with on her estate, not least because she is "not a feminist, and I really should be". "It's [*Widows*] gotten silly. They should have left it. When it was first on it was really good. You didn't know whether he was dead – it wasn't until the end that you found out he was alive. Now it's gotten silly because, I don't know, when you bring women into, I mean I'm not a feminist and I should really be, but when you start bringing women into it, it gets silly, because they don't write good enough parts for them. I mean we were watching the *Gambler* and the first two were really good – and in the last one they brought Linda Evans into it (who plays Krystal in *Dynasty*) and it got silly. It's like they are just there to look pretty, and I don't like that. She's a good actress, but she needs a good part. They write silly parts for them – to wear skimpy little costumes and to stand there looking nice – and it spoils the film. I don't like the parts they write for women in TV."

The video plays quite a central role in their family life: "We use it more or less every day." For one thing, if they really want to watch something they will videotape it and "watch it later", when their children are in bed.

Woman: "I think now the video is important for us. If we are going to watch [something videoed], if it is something we want to watch, we have put the kids to bed." For the wife, the video is a godsend in terms of keeping her children amused while she gets on with her domestic chores. "We have got about nine hours of tapes for Laura – she's three and a half. They are all things we have taped off the television – *Carebears*, *Fraggles*, *Superted* and *Smurfs*, that sort of thing, and cartoons. They are the same ones. She sits and watches over and over and over. It drives me potty, to be quite honest with you. But it's a godsend if I'm trying to do the washing or something like that, because she will just sit here and watch."

For the husband, as a shift worker, the video "comes into its own" as a means of enabling him to time-shift broadcast material which would otherwise be quite inaccessible to him. "Oh, it does make a difference. It has become part of the family. Late at night, that's when it comes into its own. Being a postman, I get up at five o'clock and most of the films come on ITV at 10.30pm until 12.30am to 1am and there is no way I can sit and watch that."

Family 12

This couple are both in their late forties and have a daughter of eighteen living with them (their son of twenty-five recently left home). Both husband and wife left school at fifteen. He works relatively well-paid shift work as a technician for British Telecom. She works part-time as a sales assistant. They live in a flat on a large council estate which they have recently bought from the council. Their flat stands out strongly (new front porch, mock-Tudor doors and leaded windows) against the run-down environment of the estate. They have lived here for twenty years and have relatives nearby. They have one colour television, one black and white set and a video. They have taken two holidays in the last year (as well as regular weekend trips to their caravan on the south coast). She is a Conservative voter. Her husband is undecided in his political views.

This couple have a seemingly contradictory set of attitudes and behaviours in relation to television. On the one hand, their set is "on all night, regardless of what is on", but they are still careful to distinguish themselves from "some people who'll watch anything". The resolution of these contradictions has to be understood in terms of how they view, and what else they do while viewing – so that while the set is on a lot they do not think of themselves as being very involved with it.

At its simplest, the wife explains that the set is "on every night – usually from when my daughter comes in at 4.30 p.m.". The only time the set goes off is when they have visitors. Otherwise it is on "regardless". "Unless someone is visiting – then we turn it off. Otherwise it is on all night, regardless of what is on. If there's nothing on then I will catch up on my serials [often soap operas that she's taped]."

None the less they clearly don't see themselves as being like "a lot of people that sit and watch TV from morning till night". This is something which they disapprove of strongly – the man on the grounds that watching television in this way (or, more precisely, watching fictional television or video in this way) is an abrogation of civic responsibility: "I don't know how they do it – not watching four hours of bloody films, you know. I mean, they don't know what's going on in the outside world, doing that."

They see their own attitude as more detached, and properly so, in relation to television and video.

Woman: "We're not that really fussed. I mean, I got a friend along the block here, they watch breakfast TV. Right the way through. They can tell you all what's on at lunchtime. I mean, they just sit there all the time in front of the television. I can't see the point. I mean, some people, like the man next door, a good friend of ours and that, but they'll watch, they'll go down the shop and they'll watch anything – I don't see the point." For this woman, watching television is also something of a luxury, or indeed a "waste of time" in relation to her sense of domestic responsibilities, her sense that she always has "got things to do". "Sometimes I can't have the television on because it just literally drives me crazy. You just sit down and you watch it, whereas you've got things to do, you know. And you can't keep watching TV. You think, 'Oh my God, I should have done this or that.'"

The wife also rather feels that her husband wastes too much time watching television ("He will never switch it off") when he could be better employed, in her view, getting on with the "decorating or something". "I'm not too fussed about it myself. I think it's an awful waste of time. Some of it is repeats. Quite a lot of it's rubbish. I think it's an awful waste of time. Especially if he has any work to do at home, decorating or something. I always say he is a TV addict. He'd have it on all day long."

For her own part, she resolves her feelings about the issue by generally doing something else while watching. "There is always something else like ironing. I can watch anything while I'm doing the ironing – I've always done the ironing and knitting and that."

Her husband's equivalent is to read while watching ("I can always read, and watch with half my attention"), but he does admit that he watches television rather more than his wife. However, his watching is a rather incidental and unfocused activity, not a particularly attentive one. "Yeah, I suppose I do, because I watch it all the time. I watch it with the little 'un, when *Blockbusters* is on and basically when I'm reading. I can virtually hear it and see it . . . but not really go into it that deep. I can read my book as well, yes. I really am a TV addict. Yes, possibly I would have it on [in the afternoon], but I wouldn't know what was going to be on, unless I looked in the paper, to see if there was anything special I wanted to watch, like a film . Otherwise it would be on, but I may be pottering about and I could keep track of it by listening and coming in and out."

This couple's tastes are quite different, and fall into the classic gender pattern (her preferring soap opera, him sport, etc.) but they have a quite well-developed *modus vivendi* that allows each partner to watch what they want, while the disinterested party tolerates this by turning to another activity. As this woman says, "He has on what he likes and I have on what I like" because "unless you have your bits on that you like, there would be arguments all the time".

Their tastes are quite different, but they can tolerate the other's foibles.

Woman: "If I put the soap operas on he will read. How he can watch those Saturday afternoon things [that is, sports programmes] I don't know. I used to like to watch *Crossroads*, because I like soap operas. He thinks it's an awful load of rubbish. He likes to watch *Auf Wiedersehen Pet* – I fall asleep in that. I can't even understand what they're talking about. I can't understand it. He's laughing and I couldn't honestly tell you about what. I find it such a strain I just fall asleep. They may as well be talking Dutch – because I don't understand it."

The key thing (as the woman explains in relation to her daughter's complaints about having sometimes to watch things she doesn't like), is an overall "contract" of mutual tolerance of differential tastes. It is of some interest that the woman identifies her son (who no longer lives there) as the person who caused difficulties in this respect – the key factor being that her son, unlike the rest of them, was a very attentive viewer ("Richard was the only one who would just sit and watch") who had failed to develop the ability to do something else while viewing, and was thus less able to tolerate programmes he didn't like because he had no other activity to turn to.

Woman: "My daughter sometimes says, 'I don't like this. Why do we have to have it on?', but I say to her, 'If we can't have this on, then when *Top of the Pops* is on then you get the same treatment,' and then she usually suffers or goes and has a shower. There used to be arguments when the boy was here. Well, he is not a boy, he's twenty-six now. He was a bit domineering. Oh, he was terrible."

This couple are very clear about which types of programmes they watch attentively, rather than in their routine mode of keeping "half an eye" on the television. For the husband it is the golf, for the wife it is *Gems*. "I can do something else while that [golf] is on, because there is a lot of walking about. But he plays golf, so he watches it."

Man: "Yes, I'm involved in it then, really plugged in. No distractions. I'm there."

Woman: "Yes, I enjoy the soap operas. Everyone thinks I'm nutty but I really enjoy them. If I think I am going to sit down for an hour and watch *Gems*, he goes 'Oh no, not *Gems*,' but then it is only an hour."

Interviewer: "And while that is on, will you just watch that?"

Woman: "Yes, I just watch that."

Again, as in a number of the other families, the woman's preference for fiction and the man's taste for factual programming also represents itself as a preference for ITV on the part of the woman and for BBC for the man, simply because these are the dominant connotations that each channel has in the viewers' minds.

Woman: "ITV, it's got to be. BBC will only go on for *Wogan* or something like that."

Man: "I watch BBC2 quite a lot." The husband here has characteristically masculine preferences in terms of programme types. In so far as he is interested in fictional material at all, it is fictional material with a realistic or "factual" base. "I like true stories – like *Sink the Bismark* or *Shogun* – that type of thing." Whereas soap opera fails to interest him at all: "I'd rather go out [of the room] than stay in and watch that". In fact, he seems on the whole to stay in the room and read.

His wife has a traditionally feminine lack of interest in things mechanical or scientific. "I don't like *Tomorrow's World*. It's a bit too involved. But you do, don't you?"

Man: "Yeah, it's magic to me." (He is a technician by trade.)

Woman: "I don't watch those. I can't understand them. I go out in the kitchen. And I cannot tolerate *Star Wars*, *Doctor Who* – science fiction things." She also shares the dislike that a number of the women in the sample have for "zany" comedy. In her case it is *Cheers* that comes in for attack: "We've never watched that *Cheers*. It's like that *Soap* – stupid. I think it was really over the top." Within the realm of comedy it is things like Felicity Kendal in *Solo* and *Butterflies* which she prefers.

Her own interests are much more rooted in a sense of locality and connection between her life experience and background and her viewing experience. "There is things you pick out in those things. There's an advertisement, and it's an opera advert on *Solo* and it's on one of her doors in *Solo*. I do some work for two men in Chelsea and one is the producer who produced the opera and I'm trying to think of what it was. It's Janet Baker in a cloak – and I say while watching, 'Oh, look it's Mr So and So's opera.' Then my sister told me if I watch the beginning of *Minder* and they are in a car park, and there is a brick wall in another scene. Well, my dad built that wall. It was filmed in Bath Road, W14. *The Sweeney* we used to watch. I think it is quite interesting to watch things set in London – although we don't watch *EastEnders*. Because sometimes you think, 'Oh I know that'. I went past Gloucester Road where they were making *Minder* and when it came on the telly I said, 'I saw that.' You get interested for that reason."

Their viewing choices are also closely interrelated with their overall leisure choices and interests. This woman's husband remarks that she is "very Royalist" and she goes on to explain that this means that "We do watch the royal programmes – and we'll get up and go to the Royal Wedding at 6 a.m." Similarly, she explains that their current viewing of swimming programmes on television derives from their own previous involvement in their children's swimming activities. "Swimming we watch. Our children used to be competitive swimmers, so we would watch the swimming. The people who swim were basically all the people we once knew. We did know a couple who went into the Olympics."

Moreover, their interest in gardening programmes and in *One Man and His Dog* is simply one part of an overall concern to escape (whether in fantasy or in reality) from the cramped urban conditions of the estate on which they live. "*Blue Peter* has got Percy Thrower in it. They've got a little garden. It's interesting. And if you follow those programmes, well, you know when not to plant and when to plant and when to pull up and when not to. I tell you another programme we forgot, *One Man and His Dog*. Oh yes. We thoroughly enjoyed that. Do you know, I'd love to move out of London. I'd give anything to move out of here and move out to somewhere much quieter, with a bit of land. We've got the caravan. You've got so much grass that side of you and that side – and that is yours. Do you know what I mean? I think, 'Oh, I'll be glad to get out of here.' So you can look on all sides. It's just a retreat to us, for the weekend. It's on a nature reserve."

As for video, it seems that it is only really important to their daughter, who would otherwise miss *Brookside* unless she was able to time-shift it (compare this preference among many other teenage girls in the sample). For this couple, while time-shifting (for example for the wife, taping afternoon soap operas to watch in the evening) plays some part in their life, renting video films certainly does not.

Man: "If there's any decent films in the video market that's good, invariably my sister gets hold of it, and if my sister gets hold of it then we get hold of it, because it comes from them to us and I will make a couple of hours' time and watch it. But that just happens. There's nothing planned about it or anything like that, you know."

Family 13

The husband here is thirty-six, his wife forty-one; they have a son of
ten and a daughter of seven. The husband left school at fifteen, his
wife at fourteen. He works as a senior caretaking officer for the local
council (and also trades in antique furniture as a sideline). She is now
a mature student, studying modern languages. They live in a very
well-furnished council flat, stuffed with books and bits of antique
furniture, and have lived there for ten years. They previously lived
only two miles away, although their nearest relatives are in other
areas of London. They have one colour television, one black and
white set and a video, and took three holidays in the last year. The
husband clearly leads a very active social life. He is a member of
various social clubs and is a Labour voter. His wife is a church-goer (a
member of the choir), a CND member, and has stood as an SDP
candidate in local elections.

Again, this family watch a lot of television, especially the wife,
who is at home more than anyone else and who watches videotapes
during the day and "things that are on in the afternoon, like
Strangers".

At weeekends viewing is quite extensive for the whole family.
"Saturday, it's on from 6am till twelve at night . . . Sunday it's right
from *Rub a Dub Dub* . . . about 7am. I can hear little feet going past in
the bedroom and the television going on. We might watch the
religious programmes, and then we go to church on Sundays, because
we are in the choir, all of us. When we come home there doesn't seem
to be very much. We might watch farming – that's quite nice to see the
farms. There isn't very much on a Sunday really except for *Supergran*.
I might watch *Songs of Praise*, you know, as we are in the choir."

Her son also watches videos before going to school, during the
week: "Nature programmes or something that was on too late."

It seems that there isn't much that they all watch together. "As a
family there's nothing we all really watch, is there? Except *Robin of
Sherwood* possibly – we do watch that, and *Supergran*. *The Young
Ones* was on last night and we would sit and be glued to that."

Indeed, of all the family the wife has the strongest interest in
television – a fact which she is quite candid about.

Interviewer: "Are there programmes that you watch and talk
about to other people or friends or whatever?"

Woman: "Oh, I drive them mad. They think I've got square eyes."
The wife spends a lot of time watching television on her own.
"Generally I'm watching on my own in here anyway. They go to bed –
he works nights – or else he's watching sport on his television. I like
Widows – now that's a thing we both sit and watch together – and
stuff like that."

In terms of power relations matters seem to fall into the usual pattern, at least at the most superficial level. When they had an automatic channel control device it was the husband who monopolised it. "Oh yes, when we had that, I never got off the chair. I nearly buckled it."

Woman: "It's like that in my parents' house actually. Dad sits there with it."

However, when we investigate matters more closely it transpires that this surface appearance of masculine power is misleading. In fact it is the wife, in this family (unlike most of those in my sample), who actually controls and plans their viewing. The explanation of this is quite simple. As a mature student this woman is acquiring a range of interests, information and confidence which place her, rather than her husband, in the dominant position in the family. Whereas in most families it is the man who scans the schedules and plans their viewing for the evening, here it is the wife who is the family's "programme controller". "No, well, I jealously guard it [the newspaper], because people read them out to me and I can't get it into sequence, you know, what order much of it is running, so I won't be separated from it. I am the programme controller." It is the wife who suggests to her husband what he might like to watch, on the basis of her reading of the schedules (although her husband does rather bridle at being "patronised" in this way). "But he doesn't know what the programme is all about and I say, 'I think you might like this,' so we give it a go and see if he likes it or not."

Man: "See, the problem is that your taste is entirely different to my taste."

Woman: "But I know what your taste is, don't I?"

Man: "Yeah, but I don't like missing anything that's good."

Woman: "Sometimes you see a title, but you don't remember what it is. You've been watching it, but you don't remember what it was about."

The same pattern clearly applies in relation to choosing videotape material to rent.

Man: "Well, she would go 'cause she'd know exactly what film to go for."

Woman: "Yes. I tell him what I've heard about it and whether he'd enjoy it."

In terms of channel preferences and programme genres the same displacement occurs. In most families the wife's preference is for ITV/entertainment programming and the husband's is for BBC/factual programming. Here these preferences are reversed. The wife refers dismissively to "rubbish" on BBC which really belongs to ITV. "You notice the rubbish creeping into the BBC now as well. *Cover Up*

- it really belongs on ITV. *Minder's* quite amusing, but I don't watch it very much. I watch it if there's nothing else."

This woman has a particularly strong preference for Channel Four, which her husband doesn't share ("I don't go straight to Channel Four, but she does.") She prefers Channel Four because it's less "stuffy" and because it doesn't "talk down to you so much". And, uncharacteristically for most of the women in my sample, she likes the style of zany comedy ("What I do like on Channel Four is *Cheers*") which she particularly associates with that channel (she also likes Lenny Henry and Kenny Everett). "I don't think they [Channel Four] talk down to you so much. And I like things like the *Young Ones* and stuff like that, and the other channels are stuffy. I mean ITV is just soap, soap and more soap generally. And Channel Four seems to be more adult - and even the films they show are much much better. What was that one about? *Eraserhead* - most unusual - I've never seen anything like that before. And that's the sort of thing you would see on Channel Four that you wouldn't see anywhere else. If there's anything new on and I don't know what it is, then I'll give it a go if it's on Four, but if it's on ITV I might not try so hard to watch it."

One way in which this woman does conform to the pattern set by the other women in the sample is in terms of viewing style. Like them, she generally does something else at the same time as viewing, and indeed has a quite precise sense of what particular programme types are compatible with which activities: "I'm at college doing modern languages, and while I'm sitting here studying I watch things like cookery and stuff like that - light stuff - but if I'm ironing I might watch things like *Wallenberg* - you know, something that I can watch."

However, in most other ways this woman is quite exceptional in my sample. For instance, in this family it is the woman who is interested in news and current affairs programming, rather than the husband. Indeed she makes some effort to interest him in material of this kind, but with little success. "We [she means "I"] like *Newsnight* very much. And *Question Time*. I might say to him, 'Look, this is about council estates in Wandsworth,' in which case..."

Man: "Yeah, then I'll watch it, but if I'm out - like sometimes I go out and I might play snooker - but if I'm sitting by myself, I'll watch *World in Action* if it's on. But I'd rather come in and watch a game of snooker than come in and watch *World in Action*. She will say, 'Let's put *World in Action* on - it's about blah blah blah...'"

Again, by contrast to the standard pattern, it is the woman rather than her husband who has an interest in science programmes. "It's the same with *Horizon*. I mean that was very interesting the other night about the lymphocytes and about how they found out how to vaccinate against the diseases and immunology. That was very interesting to me, but he would never have sat through the first five minutes."

Man: "Um, sure. No, I wouldn't have watched that. It wouldn't catch my interest."

Unlike most of the women in the sample, she has little interest in soap opera. Indeed, her husband is more interested in soap opera than she is.

Woman: "Only *Coronation Street*. *Crossroads* doesn't appeal to me - it's terrible acting. And *EastEnders*, they make me want to scream, they seem so false. *Dallas* and *Dynasty* don't appeal to me, because he's just too ridiculous, that bloke [JR]."

Man: "When she is here, I don't watch it, because I like to go out, but when she's out and there's nothing else to watch, then I watch *Dallas*. Last night I watched it, and it was very interesting really."

Because of her "masculine" tastes it is the woman in this family who experiences her preferences as different from the rest of the family, and therefore finds that "they" all talk during the programmes she is interested in. In most of the families in my sample it is the husband who has this problem, and the wife whose tastes are shared by the children. Here the positions are reversed. "If it's something I'm watching, then they all talk and chat!"

This woman also has a preference for "realistic" drama of a kind which is displayed by the men in the other families interviewed. Thus her reservations about *Wallenberg* concern precisely this point. "*Wallenberg* was so tidied up. I can't explain it. I'm sure it must have been much more chaotic than that - it just wasn't nasty enough." The point about realism is also related to her preference for "regional" programming, whether factual - "I like the six o'clock news because it's regional" - or fictional - "*Mapp and Lucia*, I love that, because we know Rye quite well. I like regional things. I think some of the Catherine Cookson books would be better on television; and *Auf Wiedersehen Pet*, and the *Likely Lads*, those sort of things ... and the *Boys from the Blackstuff*.

On the whole, the woman presents herself as having distinctively upmarket tastes: "P. D. James' thrillers they've had with Adam Dalgleish. Now they were good - *Cover Her Face* and *Expert Witness*. You see, you don't know who the murderer is till the actual ... they're fantastically complicated. They're the sort of things a person will stay and watch - they're glued to it ... I like quiz shows too, very much. *MasterMind* I enjoy and the *Busman's Holiday* is quite good as well. But those sort of things rather than the *Price Is Right*."

However, she does have to "admit" to liking some forms of what she clearly regards as "lowbrow" programming – a fact that her husband cannot resist teasing her about.

Woman: "These big productions, sometimes I watch those, you know, for pure escapism, like *Lace*. Especially, I love the long episodes. I love those."

Man: "What was that American thing that you got involved in? The photography one."

Woman: "Oh, *Cover Up*. Yes, I was involved in it, and I was shouting, 'Rubbish'."

Man: (teasing) "Yes, you were really interested in that!"

Woman: "Oh yes, and the man was very good looking!"

For the husband it is principally sports programming and crime/adventure fiction which is of interest. His interest in horse racing influences not only his viewing choices (and his use of the video) but also the family's holiday choices. As his wife wryly puts it: "Racing – he watches it, tapes it and then watches it again. There was a time when we had to take our holidays near the race courses, while the meetings were on. Yes, we've had a holiday at Cheltenham, many times."

His wife is mildly embarrassed by some of his enthusiasms, which she clearly feels are a little too "lowbrow". "He watches his sport in there – "

Man: "Yeah, it's mainly sport for me, or really good films. You've got the old ones like the *Avengers* that have come back."

Woman: "He likes things like *Goldfinger*, and stuff like that."

At first, the only kind of television programming which he will admit to talking to people about is sport ("only about sport, really") but his wife points out that his enthusiasm for London-based crime series is also a source of conversation with his friends, who move (as he does, as a part-time antiques trader) in a similar sub-culture.

Woman: "You talked to John about *Widows*."

Man: "Oh yeah, *Widows*."

Woman: "Oh, he's like a character from *Widows*, John is."

Man: "Oh, he's the *Widows*, *Fox* or *Minder* sort of routine."

Woman: "Yes, yes."

Man: "That was a good programme – *Fox*."

Woman: "Yes that was good. We know so many people who are like that."

It is this type of London-based, realistic crime fiction which he likes and identifies with strongly – and this criterion of locally based realism also has a cutting edge: it means that he is not interested in "American" stuff, precisely because it "doesn't seem real at all". "*Fox* – now that was good. *Fox*, *Widows*, it's like *Long Good Friday*. I know they are a bit nasty, but they're exciting and they're not

American. I can't relate to that American violent stuff – it doesn't seem real at all."

His wife has quite a sophisticated attitude to violence on television in relation to her concerns, as a mother, about her children's viewing. "I put my foot down on very violent films – like *Long Good Friday* – but things like the *A-Team* or *Nightrider* – no one dies in it and I don't think the children take it more seriously than they do a *Tom and Jerry* cartoon." Similarly, she is not worried about her children viewing *Grange Hill* (unlike some of the other parents in the sample) and indeed is quite in favour of it: "It's good – because they always get their come-uppance, the bad children. They always come to a sticky end. The wrong is always righted and there is a lot of anti-racism in there. It's very good, I think. It can be quite frightening to fear going to secondary school, but if you see what it could be like and the sort of things you're going to meet, it could take some of the sting out of it."

Indeed, part of the reason why she is less concerned than many of the other parents to control her children's viewing is because she feels that her children (and her young daughter in particular) are less interested in television than she is. "Well, she gets more bored with television than any of us now. You know, you say, 'Come on, Lucy, this is good,' and she'll say, 'No, I don't want to watch it.'"

As for their video, when they first had it they used to rent an awful lot of films, although they rent less now. However, as the husband puts it: "It's the Sunday afternoons that are killers. You have a glass of beer down at your local, you have your dinner about 2.30pm and then with the kids you want to watch a nice, decent film. On bad weather days we watch video if it's boring on TV. If it's a boring week we end up spending a fortune on videos."

This family do also engage in more socialised video watching. As the wife says: "His friends have got no videos – so they come round here!"

However, it is in relation to the anti-social hours which his job demands that the husband particularly appreciates the video: "I might be in the middle of a film and I can go out just like that, so the video is a life-saver – in my job you can get a call-out just for a stuck lift, and before the video you'd think it was a right – "

Family 17

The husband is thirty-nine, his wife is thirty-five and they have two ten-year old sons. The husband left school at fourteen and his wife at seventeen. He is a central-heating fitter; she is a part-time audio-typist. They live in a small council house, and have lived there for ten years, with relatives nearby. They have one colour television, one black and white set and a video, and have had one holiday in the last year. The husband was previously unemployed for some time, during which period they got badly into debt. This was also when they got their video, in order to save money by concentrating on home entertainment rather than going out. They are both Labour voters and the husband is a strong supporter of the party, although not an activist in any sense.

As in many of the other families it is the husband who is more interested in watching television. He says simply, right at the beginning of the interview, "I watch more than she does." For his wife, television is more inconsequential, on the whole: "The only time I'll ever really put it on is if I'm on my own of an evening, for company really."

In terms of viewing style this couple also fit the overall pattern of my sample. The wife tends to do other things while watching television: "I do a bit of knitting and crocheting. Eating. We sit and eat our dinner and watch telly. That's the favourite time to eat for all of us." She is conscious that her husband has a very different attitude to viewing: "When he's watching he gets very involved. I remember one Sunday he was watching and they [the children] were engrossed and involved because he was. If you're enthusiastic, they are too."

In this man's case this also involves talking while watching, but it is a form of talk directly related to the programme – a commentary to which his wife listens from the kitchen: "He gives a running commentary when I'm doing the dishes after dinner, or when I'm in the kitchen. I know what's going on on the TV. When he's with the boys I know what's going on by his running commentary."

However, the crucial point for this man is that viewing is a fairly serious and attentive business, rather than a background distraction. "I like to sit and concentrate. You lose the amosphere if the children are mucking about."

This couple are quite child-centred. Here again it is the children who are allowed to dictate programme choice, on the whole, until their bedtime.

Man: "The kids dictate it up till 9pm, though their choice is very much like ours anyway. The kids normally have a look through the paper to find out what they want to watch and then dictate to us what is watched up to 9pm."

However, once the boys have gone to bed, power passes directly to the husband. This is not because of any direct assertion on his part, but rather because his wife, in a classically feminine way, cannot bear the guilt she would feel if she were to enforce her own preferences on anyone else: "Then [when the children go to bed] he has the ultimate choice. I feel guilty if I push for what I want to see, because he and the boys want to see the same thing, rather than what a mere woman would want to watch ... If there was a love film on, I'd be happy to see it and they wouldn't. It's like when you go to pick up a video. Instead of getting a nice sloppy love story, I think I can't get that because of the others. I'd feel guilty watching it, because I'd think, I'm getting my pleasure whilst the others aren't getting any pleasure, because they are not interested."

However, her husband is clearly conscious of this problem, and goes on to explain how they try to arrive at "negotiated" solutions to conflicts of programme preference in order to give both partners some satisfaction : "If there's something like *Deer Hunter* on one side and *Airplane* on the other, we'd both plump for *Deer Hunter*, because it's got a mixture – a bit of a love story and quite a bit of action."

This couple's channel preferences are also clearly related to classic gender formations.

Woman: "Things I like least are things like *World in Action*, when it's more political. The *Money programme* – there's too much talking. On the whole I don't bother too much with those kinds of programmes. I don't like documentaries. I like something with a story, entertainment, variety." What she likes is fiction and, above all, realist fiction set in a working-class London environment: "*Widows* is the most important one – that's the one I really don't want to miss. I like to see the women coming out on top. It's so different. I really think that is a good programme. I'm not woman's lib or anything, but that is so completely different. What other programme is there where women have overruled the men? And yet, not doing it by using ... they are being sensible and ruthless and they are still as ruthless as the blokes when it comes to it. I think it is very good." (Interestingly, in contrast to most of the other men in the sample, this man also likes *Widows*: "I think it is quite interesting – I watch it.")

Beyond this very clear and particular preference for *Widows*, this woman's tastes are classically feminine. Like a number of other women in the sample she dislikes *The Young Ones* and it is the mainstream soap operas which she and her friends at work are most interested in talking about. "We sit and chat at work. The girls mainly talk about *Crossroads* and *Dynasty*. Some have missed it and want to catch up."

Her husband's tastes fit into an equally stereotyped masculine mould, with a strong preference for sports, news and current affairs, and a dislike of soap opera. "I watch sport – boxing – the *Natural World*, underwater things like that." Such things he particularly enjoys watching alone. "The things I pay least attention to are things like *Crossroads*, *Dallas* and *Dynasty*. The boys are watching

EastEnders and it doesn't interest me at all." What this man does like is factual programming and especially the news, rather than fiction. "I watch the news every day, and anything else I can find that's interesting, but there's nothing [in the way of serials] that I follow." Moreover, he would be interested in seeing even more news – on cable television, for instance. "I'd like to see a news channel – nationwide and local." It is news programming, rather than anything else, that he would talk about to his friends. "If we do talk, it'll be about something like a news programme – something we didn't know anything about, something that's come up that's interesting."

Their children's tastes again fit into the overall pattern of my findings, with *The Young Ones* coming out as a clear favourite – which the children tape. And, like a number of the other children, the video clearly plays some part in the organisation of their social life: "They watch with their friends, especially if they've taped something."

Family 18

This couple are both forty-two and have a son of eighteen living with them. Both husband and wife left school at fifteen. He is a self-employed builder with his own small company; she is a part-time playleader/helper at a local college. They are council tenants in a pleasant and well-furnished house (indeed the furnishing is quite ornate). They have lived there for three years and previously lived int the same area. They have one colour television and one black and white set and a video. They took two holidays in the last twelve months. They are both Conservative voters. The husband has clearly done quite well for himself in his chosen trade. His wife, through her college work, has rather more contact with various forms of middle-class culture, whereas her husband identifies himself as a working-class tradesman.

For this couple, television is a constant backdrop to home life. As they say, "It's on all the time basically – it normally is."

However, while it is on all the time that they're in, they are actually "in" much less than many of the other couples, as a result of the fact that their children have now grown up and become quite independent of them.

Woman: "I find we don't watch so much now the children are older. Like they are never here, so it is rather pointless us stopping indoors. When they were younger and used to be indoors, we stayed in and watched with them. My daughter doesn't even live here. The boy lives here, and then again he doesn't. He sleeps here really."

Man: "Some evenings when it is on I sit there and do invoices. We watch it periodically, because we may go out – because the kids are not here – instead of sitting indoors."

So "all the time" refers basically to the early evening period on weekdays.

Woman: "We do tape films, but we are not in very much. It's basically early in the evening we watch it, say 6.30 to 9.30pm and on Sundays. Sundays we watch the TV, we watch the film in the afternoon. I always have the Sunday service on, the Harry Secombe thing – I quite like that."

Again we see the need to consider the joint operation (and interaction) of the factors of programme preferences and time availability (as dictated by domestic and work obligations). "*Minder* we watch regular – and *Coronation Street*, we always have that on, because 7pm we finish tea and we come up here and sit down. Switch on the TV. It's on, so you automatically watch it."

In this couple, again the husband seems to assume a position of power in relation to programme choice and, as his wife puts it, he does so quite unconsciously: "He's very good at doing that – getting up and turning the telly over, even if the adverts are not on. If he is laying on the floor and he gets fed up with it, you could be really engrossed in it, without him knowing, and he will get up and switch it over. I say, 'Hey, I was watching that,' and he says, 'That was a bit boring.'"

From the husband's point of view it seems that the presence of his son constitutes the main source of conflict over programme preferences which he is aware of. "We watch *World in Action* and those sorts of programmes, but if my son is here we tend not to have that on, because he will be watching something else."

In terms of viewing styles this couple replicate the basic pattern of my sample, with the men tending towards a more attentive style of viewing (although he does refer to sometimes doing invoices in front of the TV) and the women being less interested in television and feeling that "just watching" without doing something else at the same time is a "waste of time". "I knit because I think I am wasting my time, just watching. I know what is going on and so I only have to glance up. I always knit when I watch."

Man: "I can really get involved if it is a film or a documentary on animals – then I am well away."

Woman: "That is more the time when we talk – in a documentary – but if it is a film we don't normally. Well, he doesn't, but I do. Because I find TV boring."

Similarly their tendencies, both in terms of how much they talk to people about television at all and in terms of which types of programming they talk about, fit the classic pattern of sex role stereotyping.

Woman: "I'll talk about things to my friends. I do. I think it is women who talk about TV more so than men! I work with an Indian girl and when *Jewel in the Crown* was on we used to talk about that, because she used to tell me what was different in India. *Gandhi* we had on video. She told me what it was like, and why, and that was interesting. Other than that, it is anything. She went to see *Passage to India* and she said it was good, but it was a bit like *Jewel in the Crown*."

Man: "I won't talk about TV at work unless there had been something like boxing on. I wouldn't talk about *Coronation Street* or a joke on *Benny Hill*, so other than that, no."

The wife expresses a fundamental channel loyalty to ITV: "We mainly watch ITV. We very rarely watch Channel Four. My son does and he tapes Channel Four. It doesn't enter my head to switch on Channel Four."

Her husband is quick to point out that not only does he like current affairs programmes on ITV (rather than entertainment programmes) but that he also watches that type of material on BBC ("except the political ones"). "I like *World in Action*. We do watch BBC – *Panorama*. I find those very entertaining, except the political ones. I like all the world event things."

His wife's preferences centre on entertainment programmes, in a classically feminine mould. "*Thornbirds* – I thought that was really good. We like the best-sellers. I always watch them or get them taped. They are quite harmless. *Wallenberg* was the last one!"

Again, like a number of other women interviewed, she is a great fan of *Widows* – to the extent of watching the repeat showing of the series as well. "We even watched when they showed it again – and the ones we couldn't watch we swopped with people who were taping them, so we could see them before the new series. It was good. Ken did once say that they looked like lesbians – just because it is women." Her preference for *Widows* seems to be related to a criterion of realism that also provides her rationale for choosing between different soap operas – and for preferring those set in a more realistic, British context. "Out of the soap opera things I watch *Crossroads* and *Coronation Street*. I don't watch *Dallas* or *Dynasty*. I think they have had their day."

Conversely, it is the same criterion which leads her husband to dismiss *EastEnders*: "It's supposed to be everyday life in the East End. It's supposed to be what the East End was not so long ago. That is the impression I got, but I have only seen it once. I think the slang is overdone – a lot of the slang words are nothing to do with cockney. I don't know who the scriptwriter is. He needs to be shot. Even the missus in the pub, I mean who would go to a pub with the missus staggering around like that? It's stupid."

This man likes *Coronation Street* and *Minder*, which presumably "pass" his criterion of "realism", but, as for *Eastenders*: "I think it is overplayed. It's pathetic. I watch that Jim Davidson – *Up the Elephant and Castle*."

In the same vein as Jim Davidson the humour of ITV's game shows appeals to him strongly. "*The Price is Right*, that's a good programme, isn't it? Some of the prizes they give are very good. We always watched *Game for a Laugh*."

Both parties in this couple also have their own personal viewing interests – which relate for the woman to her other leisure interests. "I watch things on health – I'm a bit health conscious. I used to run a slimming club and I swim quite a lot, so if they are going to have anything on about what you should and shouldn't eat, I'll look out for that."

And for her husband, to his work (as a carpenter and builder): "They used to have a do-it-yourself programme on a Sunday morning I would normally watch that – there is always good tips in that." And as regards his hobby (collecting antique clocks): "I used to like the *Antiques Roadshow* on a Sunday."

As in most of the families, their video is particularly significant for their teenage son's social life.

Woman: "He tapes all the music programmes – then he can watch on his own at whatever time. His friends come and watch together – they have their tapes. My son uses it a lot. We have never got any tapes here, because he has used them and they are always at his friend's house."

Interestingly the wife, like a number of the other women interviewed, also organises social viewing with her women friends around the video. "I don't work Mondays, and quite often my friends will get a film and watch it up here. I have done that about three times. A lot of my friends haven't got videos – they can't afford them. So it is something special to them."

(iii) C_1 Families

Family 9

This couple are both in their mid-thirties, with a son of sixteen and daughters of fourteen and twelve. Both husband and wife left school at fifteen. He is a self-employed retail salesman (selling fashionable "designer" sweatshirts and trainers); she is a full-time cook superviser. They are owner-occupiers in a house they have bought on a modern council estate. They have lived here for eleven years, previously living only one mile away, and have relatives living within a few hundred yards. They have one colour television, one black and white set and a video. They took one holiday in the last year. Their flat is very well furnished and the whole family clearly benefits from the husband's access to fashionable clothes. The husband is a keen snooker player and is a member of two pool teams. His son is also a keen player and one wall is stacked with the snooker trophies that father and son have won. The wife is a member of a local darts team. He is a Labour voter, but his wife does not vote (indeed she has no interest at all in national politics).

Once again it is the husband who has the greater interest in television and seems to watch it rather more than his wife, who is interested in very few programmes apart from "down to earth" soap operas.

Woman: "I don't like TV. It's very rare ... it's got to be something very good that I want to see. It bores me. Truthfully. He's the one that likes the TV. When he goes out it won't be on."

Man: "I watch telly – quite a bit of the time. If I'm in I'll always have the telly on. I go out a couple of nights a week, but the nights I stay in I do watch the television. If I come in from work I turn on the TV. It's like a habit."

Woman: "Whereas I'll put the records on. It's got to be something really good for me to put the telly on.'

On occasion her husband tries to stimulate her interest in what television has to offer, but seems to meet with little success.

Man: "Like last night, I mean I was sitting down here on my own and the old lady was doing things – ironing or something or other – and there was a film on and it was a sad film, you know, and I knew my wife would like it, and I was trying to tell her about it, but she wouldn't take no notice."

The relations of power in the family assume a very traditional form, symbolised by the husband's use of the automatic control device.

Daughter: "It's always next to Daddy's chair. It doesn't come away when Dad's here. It stays right there."

Woman: "And that's what you do, is it? Yes, flick, flick, flick when they're in the middle of a sentence on the telly. He's always flicking it over."

Interviewer: "Do you use it a lot?"

Man: "What, the remote control? Oh yes, I use it all the time."

Daughter: "Well, if you're in the middle of watching something, Dad's got a habit of flicking over to the other side to see the result of the boxing."

Equally, this family also seems to display the same pattern of gender differences in relation to viewing style observed elsewhere in my sample, with the man claiming a strong preference for attentive silent viewing, which he feels is disturbed by his wife and daughters, although his wife disputes this account of what happens.

Woman: "Every now and again he says, 'Shut up!' It's terrible. One minute they're – say we're listening to something, and he's come home from a pool match and he'll say, 'Shut up! Please shut up!' "

Man: "You can't watch anything in peace unless they're all out. Half the time they start an argument and then you've missed easily twenty minutes of it, usually the catchphrase which you've got to listen to to find out what's going to happen in the programme. Sometimes I just go upstairs. It's not worth watching. This house isn't a quiet house, as you can see, with her butting in. It usually isn't a quiet house."

Interviewer (to woman): "So it'd be you who'd be doing the nattering, is that it?"

Man: "Yes, it is her normally."

Woman: "When you [the man] come in, no one can listen to nothing because he has to tell the world what's gone outside."

Man: "No, I like to watch it without aggravation. I'd rather watch on me own – if it's just something I want to watch, I like to watch everything with no talking at all."

Apart from the question of viewing style, when one considers the question of programme preferences it becomes clear that the wife's central preference is not simply for soap opera, but for "down to earth" soap opera.

Woman: "Soap opera's all right. That's what I watch, just the soap operas. Down to earth things. I like *EastEnders, Coronation Street* – oh, and *Widows*."

Later, she expands the point, explaining that what she likes is seeing "different things going on in different families". "I like the doctors' programmes. I like them – *The Practice*, 'cause that's a little bit like a saga an' all, isn't it? – different things. I like different things going on in different families. I like all that. Sagas – like *Blockbusters*, *The Winds of War, From Here to Eternity*."

While she mentions a preference for some elements of more "romantic" programming ("tearjerkers"), her basic criterion that a programme must be "down to earth" means that she is no great fan of *Dallas* or *Dynasty*, which fail the test on this criterion, as they are not considered realistic and are not set in urban, working-class areas. "*Dallas* and *Dynasty* are far-fetched. It's all romantic things in it. I think it's far-fetched. I think it's ridiculous. I don't think anybody goes around like they do. Although I watch it, I think it's really far-fetched. I don't want anybody to be so bloody rich. I tell you what I did love when it was on – we loved *Roots*. We watched that. That was down to earth, that was."

Like a number of other women in the sample, she expresses a liking for "tear-jerkers" (elsewhere referred to as "a nice weepie"). "I like tear-jerkers, things that are really sad, more so than anything funny, 'cause I don't like things funny. I like, really, tear-jerkers – something like *Thornbirds*. Yes, I loved that one, it was great."

Her distaste for comedy is, as she indicates, somehow associated with a distinctively feminine dislike of the particular kind of zany and disruptive humour which her teenage children appreciate so much. "Kenny Everett can't make me laugh. Lenny Henry don't make me laugh. You see, I don't find all that funny really."

It may be that she does not find this material funny precisely because of the way in which it represents and validates domestic disorder, which of course reaches its apogee in *The Young Ones*, of which she says: "That's sickly. I think they're real sick. If that's on, I do the washing, anything."

With regard to news and current affairs programming she appears to be quite disinterested in national news programming because of her feeling that it is about events which she does not understand and has no practical relation to. Whereas she does have an interest in local news, precisely in so far as she feels that it connects with her own interests, her own understanding and her role as a mother. Current affairs programming she dismisses out of hand. "I can't stand all this *World in Action* and *Panorama* and all that. It's wars all the time. You know, it gets on your nerves." News programming, at a national level, she is only slightly less dismissive of. "What I read in the papers and listen to the news is enough for me. I don't want to know about Chancellor somebody in Germany and all that. When I've seen it once I don't want to see it again. I hate seeing it again – 'cause it's on at breakfast time, dinner time, tea time. You know, the same news all day long, it bores me. What's going on in the world? I don't understand it all, so I don't like to listen to that. I watch – like those little kids – that gets to me. I want to know about it. Or if there's actually some crime in Wandsworth, like rapes and all the rest of it –

I'd want to read up on that, if they'd been caught and locked away. As for like the guy says the pound's gone up and the pound's gone down, I don't want to know about all that – 'cause I don't understand it. It's complete ignorance really. If I was to understand it all I probably would get interested in it."

Her only positive comments are precisely in relation to local news: "Sometimes I like to watch the news if it's something that's gone on – like where that little boy's gone and what's happened to him. Otherwise I don't, not unless it's local – only when there's something that's happened." And her preference for local news of this type is associated with an interest in *Help* and *Crimewatch*, in so far as they relate to her concerns over her family's safety and well-being.

While her husband is no great fan of news and current affairs programming, he is slightly less alienated from material of this type and may occasionally watch documentary programmes "if there's nothing else on".

Man: "I wouldn't turn it on to watch it – you know what I mean? But if it was there, I sometimes get interested in it, and I'd watch it then. I wouldn't plan for it, but some of them are quite interesting." However, he is most interested in sport and light entertainment. This is why he expresses a preference for ITV as a channel – because ITV is associated in his mind with "the type of things" he likes. The only exception he notes is sport (which is what he is most interested in), where his choice of BBC is a consequence of his preferred style of uninterrupted, attentive viewing.

"I think we tend to watch ITV in general, because there's on the whole better things on ITV. I think so anyway. You get more series like – the type of things that we like – like *Sweeney* or *Minder*. It's normally ITV, isn't it? Things like the *Fame Game*, *Dynasty*, *Family Fortunes*, *Blockbusters*, things like that . . . But when it comes to sport, if there's a cup final on both sides, I'll always choose BBC, because there's no interruptions."

The man's other strongly expressed preference is for American programmes in general, which probably derives from his own cultural formation as a "mod" (still evident in his own style of dress as an adult): a culture which emphasised American commercial culture as the key source of style for British working-class youth. Interestingly, his preference for American television contrasts strongly with his wife's dismissal of American soap opera as "far-fetched". Clearly, the question of their "realism" or otherwise is not the central issue for him. "I like *Dallas* or *Dynasty* when they're on. Like my wife said, you can always catch up on them. I don't like *Crossroads* and *Coronation Street*."

Woman: "*Dallas* and *Dynasty* are far-fetched."

Man: "That's it, I like them better. I do. American TV is much better than English."

He and his son express a liking for *Only Fools and Horses*, his son linking that preference to one for *Minder*. However, his son is careful to make it clear that while he likes these programmes, television viewing as an activity is itself not a priority for him if it conflicts with the opportunity to be out, engaging in "real" activity. "I like *Minder* and *Only Fools and Horses*, but if I'm out I wouldn't come back and watch them."

However, in the case of sport (and only in that case), his father will "make a point" of watching it on television, even if it means coming home specially for the purpose.

Man: "If there's sport on – football, boxing – I make a point of getting home to watch it." Equally, sport is the only form of television which the father will admit to talking about with friends or workmates: "It'd be boxing I might talk about – sport – football – or if there's a big fight coming up we discuss who you think is going to win."

He is also more attentive to sports programming because he is a snooker player himself (with a wall full of trophies) and feels he may well be able to improve his own technique by studying closely the professionals on television. "Sometimes in snooker when they pot a ball, they hit it in the pocket so hard and the white runs off the cushion about a centimetre, and you think, I wonder how they do that. And you try ways to try and do it."

Interviewer: "So you might be learning shots from watching them, as well as just enjoying it?"

Man: "Oh yes, you definitely learn. You learn to always keep your head down – what side of the ball to hit the white on when you want it to go a certain way, and all that. It definitely improves your game, yes."

Like her brother, the family's eldest teenage daughters on the whole prefers other activities (in her case listening to music) to watching television: "I like *Top of the Pops*, *Saturday Superstore*, things like that. But I wouldn't really stay in to watch telly. I prefer to turn it off and listen to records."

These teenagers are keen fans of zany comedy and of *The Young Ones* in particular: "We definitely like comedies the best – the *Kenny Everett Show*, *The Young Ones*. I can't get over how briliant that is. *Lenny Henry* – that's brilliant. *Three of a Kind* – that was good, but I think it's a new kind of comedy. It should have been done before. I think it's brilliant. I like the way they break it up and it gets very kind of surrealistic – the fridge starts talking and all that. I know it's daft, but I like it."

"At our school they always talk about the telly and videos and what they tape, and it's mostly things like *The Young Ones*."

Their enthusiasm leads them to use their video in order to repeat-view the series – preferably during holidays, or when their parents are out, so as not to have their enjoyment marred by their mother's disdain (a relatively common use of video in my sample – to time-shift "contentious" material to a point where it can be watched in the "best" context).

Daughter: "We've got a tape of *The Young Ones*, right through this series till now. We always watch it."

Mother: "The kids do when I'm out. They know every word of it. It bores me. They sit and watch it again and again."

Daughter: "It's so brilliant."

Father: "It keeps them quiet for hours, watching."

Here it is the teenagers who use the video in this "social" way more than anyone else, although their parents also do so on occasion.

Woman: "Yes, last week or the week before some friends of ours came and watched *Widows*. They forgot to tape it and they asked if we was taping it and we said yes, so they came round the following day..."

The couple's relationship to the video recorder is fairly standard for my sample. The man goes to the video shop to hire tapes and is generally the active user of the machine. His wife doesn't use it at all herself. She explains that she is unable to use it, as she doesn't understand it. "I can't use it. I tried to tape *Widows* for him and I done it wrong. He went barmy. I don't know what went wrong."

Family 14

The husband is twenty-seven years old, his wife twenty-six, with a daughter of six and a son of five from her previous marriage. Both husband and wife left school at sixteen. He is a caretaker on a local estate; she is currently trying to start up her own small business. They own their small flat and have lived here for just over a year. The flat is furnished in a very "modern" and stylish manner (hand-painted stencils on the wall, low-level seating, tubular steel fittings, etc.). They both previously lived in the same area, though their relatives live some distance away. They have one colour television set and a video, and took one holiday in the last year. He is a member of a local darts team and she of a local health club. Although the husband had previously been a life-long Labour supporter, he voted Conservative in the last election and says that he would probably do so again (though with growing doubts). His wife is a firm supporter of the Conservative Party.

This couple are not greatly interested in television at all. This is evident from the layout of their sitting-room: the set itself is a small portable and the room is not so clearly organised around the set as it is in most homes. They explain that they don't watch it that much, except when their "TV fanatic" friend from upstairs drops in.

Woman: "We've got a friend who comes round who is a television fanatic, so we watch when she's around. It's on, but..."

Man: "I just read the paper to see. And we might say there's something good on around 7.30 or 8pm – and we might turn it on weekends. We don't watch much. Sundays, only if there's a decent film on. Otherwise it stays off."

The woman explains that she only got a television set at all for her young daughter's sake. "I only got this – and I wasn't going to bother with a TV, to be quite honest – but I got it for my daughter, 'cause my daughter used to come up from school and sit and watch it and it seemed to unwind her, so I got one for her, more than anything. Only obviously now I use it. To start off with I wasn't even going to bother –especially as my son isn't interested."

The woman's remarks about how much television her kids watch when they visit their father from whom she is divorced, points even more strongly to the contrast with the ethos of this household, in which television has quite a marginal place. "When they go to their father's they watch TV and video a lot – 'cause they come back and talk about everything."

This couple hire video films more regularly than most of the other couples in my sample: "at weekends we tend to get two or three". They also are the only couple I interviewed who seem to go to the cinema regularly, which could be partly explained by the fact that they have the opportunity to do so when the children visit their father and they are freed from baby-sitting problems. However, this would not explain the lack of cinema-going among the other families in my sample with older children who don't need baby-sitting.

Woman: "I love going to the cinema. We went to see *Brazil* on Saturday. We've been to see lots of films. I prefer going up to Leicester Square, to the big screen. We saw *Raiders of the Lost Ark* – all Spielberg's films. *Poltergeist*."

When asked about the television programmes they particularly like, they both referred to programmes where the point about them was, as far as they were concerned, their realistic portrayal of an urban working-class environment with which they both identify strongly. For the man it is *Only Fools and Horses* which best provides this particular satisfaction, and is the source of his strongest enthusiasm: "Oh, it's superb – the best programme that's ever been on TV I think. Just perfect – very, very natural – so realistic – 'cause a lot of people I know, or used to know – I could see certain characters – you know, people I know. I just crack up. Oh God, yes."

For the woman, it is *Widows* which is her favourite. Her strong enthusiasm for it is all the more striking given her lack of interest in most television programmes. In this case she is even prepared to rearrange her work commitments around the scheduling of the programme: "*Widows*. I like it. Everybody seems to be ... like people I work with! It's got the atmosphere. If you go in a pub you can meet the characters. I can believe it. I can actually relate to *Widows*. I think it's very believable – I can really see the situation. Somebody taped it [the series] so it was six hours we sat and watched – lovely, like all night – brilliant. I didn't want it to end. We swop nights off so's I won't miss it, because it doesn't bother me if I miss most things, but it'd be different if I missed *Widows*. That's probably the only programme."

As in a number of other families in my sample, it is only the man who routinely checks the television schedules in order to plan viewing choices. As the woman explains: "I don't read newspapers. If I know what's going to be on, I'll watch it. He tends to look in the paper. I don't actually look in the papers to see what's on."

However, in contrast to most of the other families, here it is the man who characteristically talks while viewing, and the woman who objects.

Man: "Normally I will talk, but she doesn't like me talking. If *Widows* is on, I'm not allowed to talk, but normally we don't sit here glued to it, I'll talk while I watch it."

More routinely, in terms of programme preferences the man talks of having the predictable masculine interest in "factual" programming, but explains that while he used to watch programmes of this type (when living alone) he rarely does so now, because of his wife's dislike of them. "I like the science programmes. I *would* watch them, but she's watching something else. I always used to watch the documentaries and that, but since we got together I don't watch them so much. I would if I were on my own."

Like other men in the sample, not only does he watch sport on television enthusiastically, but, as a darts player himself, has a particular interest in studying the techniques of the players: "Mostly rugby and athletics – that's compulsory! Snooker I watch quite a bit. Darts – last year John Lane got a darts sequence and the camera zoomed up. That was really interesting, watching how he went for the sequence."

In one sense his wife's preferences and attitudes fall into line with those of most of the women in the sample. For instance, she explains that she has no interest in news or current affairs programming, whereas "I could watch those epics – with Charlton Heston and things, *Ben Hur* and all that kind of stuff. I love it." In the same vein, she explains that she enjoys *Dynasty* and only watches television on Saturdays because of it: "*Dynasty*, I can watch that – I love it. But if that wasn't on we wouldn't be watching on a Saturday night, would we? We wouldn't switch it on."

However, in other respects she is quite uncharacteristic of the women in my sample. For one thing, she is a fan of *The Young Ones*, which most of the other women in my sample dislike strongly, even though she claims she would not put the television on specially to watch it. "I like *The Young Ones*, of course. Though I don't actually – I never turn the TV on to watch it." Moreover, despite claiming to enjoy *Dynasty* she also talks very disparagingly about soap opera in general (and of women who get really "involved" in it), rather in the way in which many of the men in the sample dismiss soap opera: "I used to actually work with somebody who was an absolute ... well, there was two of them – *Dallas* fanatics – and they used to be so worked up about it, it was untrue. God, it was like their life – they used to get so ratty about J.R. It was incredible – I just couldn't believe that anyone could really be into that series. It's as though they were talking about their family and, really, it seemed to me that – I can't stand some of it. They watch *Emmerdale Farm* and *Coronation Street*! You can't really talk about it."

This seems to be a statement about what "one" can and can't talk about with reference to some standard of social acceptability. This may have a particular relevance for her, as a working-class woman who is trying to set up her own business and move upwards socially. This may also explain why she then speaks so guiltily of her own pleasures in reading "pulp" novels, as pleasures which she feels are not really appropriate to someone with her social ambitions. "I don't use the library, but I like reading. The last few months I haven't read but at one time I was reading two books a week. I used to be a receptionist and then I used to read about four books a week! But I read a lot of crap and all the scandal stuff – Harold Robbins and all that. The last one I really enjoyed, which I shouldn't have done, was *Lace*. I read it from cover to cover."

Beyond the question of class this is also a matter of feminine guilt, which is shared by many of the other women in the sample who are guilty about their fictional pleasures, given the low status that these are given within the culture.

Family 15

The husband is thirty, his wife twenty-eight; they have sons of six and three. The husband left school at fifteen, his wife at sixteen. Both are now self-employed: he runs his own painting and decorating business, she is setting up a small hairdressing salon. They are private tenants in a small, comfortable house in a quiet street. They have one colour television (with teletext), one black and white set and a video. They took two holidays in the last year. She is a spiritualist and reads extensively in this field. He says that he barely reads at all (not even newspapers since they got teletext). He votes Labour. She is a supporter of the Ecology Party.

Again it is the man who watches television more than his wife: "Yes, I watch it more than she does." This, as his wife explains, is partly to do with the fact that her circumstances have changed, as she is now setting up her own business. "I used to watch it a lot but not now, because I've got a business going and I'm in and out all the time. He's at home all the while. I'm out evenings on business and visiting friends."

The woman watches some afternoon television of a relatively "serious" type, compared with her husband's "lowbrow" tastes, by which she is slightly embarrassed. "Occasionally I watch it of an afternoon, if there's something I want to watch. There's one particular programme I quite like of an afternoon – *Sarah Kennedy*." Later she explains that her viewing at that time of the evening has to be organised around her domestic obligations. "You see I'm watching about that time – 5 to 6pm really, isn't it? That's when I'm watching it, because the children are usually eating their tea, and I can just sit down and watch it with them. Afterwards, I'm usually in here in time for *Coronation Street*."

Generally it is a household in which the television set is simply on all evening, from the point where the children return from school, whether or not anyone is actively viewing.

Man: "It goes on when the children come in from school, and then it's on for the rest of the night. Even if we're not watching it, it's there. Sometimes it's on and I'm over there [that is to say, out of sight of the screen] and she's in the kitchen. It's just on."

Woman: "Or I'll be sitting reading and he's sitting reading the paper and it's just on. I can generally sit and read a book and watch a film at the same time and keep the gist of it, if it's a good film. It doesn't bother me."

Interviewer: "Do you do that a lot, do something else while you are watching?"

Woman: "Yes, quite a lot, sewing or something like that."

Interviewer: "Or you will leave the sound up and vaguely follow it from the kitchen?"

Woman: "Yes, especially if it's something I like keeping a track of."

Their viewing is fundamentally unplanned on the whole.

Whereas, in many of the families, the husband at least will check the television schedules in the paper to plan viewing choices, the fact that this man in fact uses teletext to replace the paper's function makes viewing even more incidental. He is clearly a channel-hopper (to his wife's mild chagrin) and it is he rather than his wife who uses the automatic control device which controls the teletext and channel functions. "It just goes on, and we all watch whatever comes on and flick it back if it's something we don't like. I flick about the channels and watch something for a couple of seconds and if there is nothing on either side, that's all I do, and mess about and try to find something that is what I want to watch."

Interviewer: "Do you use the automatic control? Do you sit there with it next to you?"

Woman: "No, not really. I leave that down to him. It is aggravating sometimes because you can be watching something and all of a sudden he turns it over to get a football result."

Man: "I put the teletext on to get the results during the game. I'm a teletext addict. We rarely buy the papers now we've got the teletext." He goes on to explain that he uses the teletext facility quite a lot: "Especially when there is nothing else on at all – I just mess about with it. Like the news, or whatever, all things like that – the stars, jokes."

When it comes to programme preferences, this man's tastes are for popular (mainly ITV) programmes, especially quizzes: "I like the quiz programmes – *Question of Sport* and things like that. *MasterMind*, I don't like that very much, and we don't watch that very often, mainly because we don't get the questions right. You get disheartened after a bit! Same with *University Challenge*. We like *Blockbusters* – that's good, isn't it? And the children like that as well."

He explains that both he and his wife enjoy the popular soap operas: "*Coronation Street* and *Dallas* we are quite hooked on." But some tension arises between the couple as the man explains how much he likes *The Price is Right*. His wife is slightly better educated than him and regards her husband's tastes as embarrassingly "lowbrow".

Man: "*The Price is Right* is my favourite – I like that one."

Woman: "I find that ... I think I'd get quite embarrassed actually, going on a programme like that!"

Man: "She's not a great lover of that!"

The basis of this tension is referred to again in an oblique way when discussion turns to matters of literacy.

Woman: "He doesn't even want to fill in forms, I've got to read them out."

Man: "I've never been to a library. I can't read a book or anything. The only thing I can read is the paper – that's as far as I go. If they put a book on the telly, I'll watch it."

This also lies behind the following discussion with the woman in relation to her partiality for "police" series. Her criterion for liking them is that they "get your brain working", but she is slightly edgy about the particular series under discussion (P. D. James), which she actually found too difficult to follow, despite feeling that it was "very good".

Woman: "I tend to like the 'police' ones, trying to fathom out who's done it."

Interviewer: "So did you watch things like that P. D. James' serial, *Cover Her Face?*"

Woman: "Yes, I tried to, but I didn't like it, and I kept switching it off! I got bits and pieces of that, and of course it was on Sunday night, and we had visitors that time to watch our video you see, so it was on and off, and on and off and I was catching bits of it. I found that very good, actually, I like a whodunit. It gets your brain working."

Her husband's tastes in fiction focus on series which are set firmly in working-class areas of London, with which he clearly identifies strongly: "*Minder*, I always watch *Minder*. Yes, I like that. The best one I like is *Only Fools and Horses*. It's very good that – and *The Bill* we like, don't we? We always watch that."

It is the same criterion, but here operating negatively, which leads his wife to reject *EastEnders* as unrealistic and failing to offer her an acceptable point of identification: "I find some of the accents rather over the top, really too much. I don't think it's what I think the East End is like. I've only really been there a couple of times, but – especially the pub life and all that – there's all this carrying on all the time, you know. That to me isn't – I know it happens in life, but it's not true to life, if it's supposed to be a soap opera. True to life, it wouldn't be as much as what's in there."

When discussing *Coronation Street* (which they both watch), this woman points out that this programme is, in her view, more realistic and does provide characters which she can relate to – although she is careful to qualify this by pointing out that she doesn't get too involved, "like some people do". "Some of it, yes. Some of the characters just make me laugh, you know, and that's what I think it should be. I can see some of the things happening that happen in that part of it tickles me. You can get involved in it, because you can actually relate to the characters, some of them. I don't mean I get that involved – like some people do, you know, when people pass away. You know, they get killed off and people send wreaths and that. I think they get too involved."

Similarly, she is faintly embarrassed by having to admit that she enjoys *Quincy* (despite feeling that it is "pathetic in some ways") which she refers to one of the few American programmes which they watch at all: "*Miami Vice* is about the only American programme we really watch, isn't it? And *Dallas*. Oh, except for my *Quincy*, I do love *Quincy*. It's quite pathetic in some ways, but I still like it. He sits there groaning."

Man: "I taped it for her last night, but I didn't watch it."

In terms of channel loyalty, the woman's clear preference is for ITV (or for BBC programmes which are close to her image of "ITV-type" programmes), like most of the women in my sample: "I think *Dallas* is the only regular programme that we watch on BBC. *EastEnders* I've started to watch lately, but I don't think much of it. We rarely watch Channel Four. Very rarely. Tuesday nights I like their films, but other than that, no."

Her attitude to news programming also fits in with the standard feminine pattern in my sample of preferring local news above all: "*Reporting London* – more than anything in the news sort of line we watch that. That's what's happening where we're living, in the city."

When asked if there are television programmes which they'd talk about to anyone, the main point the husband makes is that he would be more likely on the whole to discuss video films (possibly because that is more like talking about something "special" like going to the cinema) rather than broadcast television programmes. "It's mainly videos I'll talk about. To discuss telly, that'd be very occasionally." occasionally."

The wife says that she might discuss a television programme related to her special interest (spiritualism), but also goes on to refer to the value of programmes like *Dallas* as a talking point in social situations.

Woman: "If there's a discussion programme on, especially the Arthur C. Clarke one ... I think *Dallas* is the best talking point, especially with people who don't like it! Our friend who comes in on a Sunday night doesn't like and his wife does and we do. We talk about it and we do it really just to annoy him, to aggravate him ..."

More centrally, it is *Only Fools and Horses* which is singled out as a "common ground" for talk – further evidence of the widespread enthusiasm for the programme in areas such as this. Woman: "I think the real talking point is about *Only Fools and Horses* when that's on. You hear people talking about that all over the school. It's quite a well-liked programme. Well, especially as my eldest boy's name is Rodney – and he loves it and everyone starts calling him 'Rodders' now, they all call him Rodders over at school!"

When asked about their use of the video recorder, it becomes clear both that they use it a great deal (like most of the families in the sample mainly for time-shifting purposes, although this couple regularly hire films on a Sunday night) and that it is mainly the husband who uses it, although often in order to tape things for his wife.

Man: "Nearly every night we tape something. We do use it a lot. I use it and then I tape a lot of things for her. I usually watch them and tape them for her."

However, this woman does use the video herself to some extent – in order to view "love stories" (which she knows her husband doesn't like) while he's out of the way: "I get one of those if he's not in."

Man: "Yes, I don't want to sit through all that."

Woman: "It's on his nights out. It doesn't happen very often."

Like many of the mothers in the sample, she has also become aware of the advantages and uses of the video as a way of "keeping the children quiet". "We get them a film from the shop – keeps them quiet for a few hours." Their children's friends also come round to watch, so that their viewing is quite often a social occasion. "The eldest once does, yes, they do come and watch tapes. But generally they come in here because they tape *Masters of the Universe* and the kids are into that at the moment. They're mad about it, even the little girls – I was quite surprised. They'll have friends in and watch that. They know everything what's going to happen – he does this and he does that – and they're all still watching it."

This couple have a well-established routine of having friends round to watch a video in company: "Every Sunday – we have for years, we always have a video. Our friends come round and he always brings one with him. We've been doing that for years."

With regard to broadcast television, the wife is particularly conscious of having her own very personal interests, partly as a matter of her own professional interest as a hairdresser: "I like the period costumes and things like that. It fascinates me especially when they go back over time and you can see the various different hairstyles. Then I watch those, but it is mainly trying to find a fault in them, what they have done, if the hair doesn't suit the costume they have got on." But also in terms of her own personal leisure activity, as a spiritualist. This has a positive effect on her television choices: "I like the Arthur C. Clarke series – we usually tape that and watch it, and tape it as well so that we can watch it again." But it also has a negative effect in terms of how this leisure interest precludes not viewing certain programmes: "Well I am a spiritualist, and I won't watch horror films that are to do with the supernatural that to me are ridiculous. He still loves them, but I can't, because I think it is ludicrous. How can they make something like that? They don't even know what they are talking about. So that does affect what I watch."

(iv) B Families

Family 4

Both husband and wife are in their early forties. They have a daughter of thirteen and they also have the husband's sixty-eight-year-old mother living with them. Both husband and wife stayed at school until they were nineteen. He is a furniture dealer and she is now a mature student of law. They own their spacious and well-furnished house and have lived here for ten years (moving here from across the road). They have relatives living within a mile. They have three colour televisions, one black and white set and a video, and took one holiday in the last year. The husband used to be a traditional folk singer. He is now a local history enthusiast and is a member of the local Historical Society. The wife is a member of both the Local Residents' Association and the Labour Party. Her husband is a committed non-voter. His strongest sense of self-identification is as a "Cockney born and bred" who has made his own way up the ladder of success.

The basic viewing pattern for this couple is, like most of the other families in this social category, to view later in the evening.

Man: "We don't tend to watch until about 9pm. I tend to look in the paper and see what's on for, say, 9.30pm." However, this pattern is slightly skewed in the household by the fact that the husband's elderly mother also lives with them and she also watches both *TV-am* and early evening television. The husband explains that at these times the main set in the living-room is on a lot – because of his mother and their teenage daughter ("the professional watcher") and someone will always be watching at some point. "My mother comes in about 5pm and puts it on, and I don't watch until 7, or 7.30pm." Of himself he says, "I sit and read a book and turn the sound down. There's always someone watching with four people in the house. I like Sunday afternoons, because everyone's out and I go upstairs and read."

Basically this man is defensive about watching television at all: "I won't just put it on to see what's on. I'm not usually here. I watch it if there's nothing else to do, but I'd rather not."

Earlier, his wife has explained that she watches television "slightly less than normal" because she's studying in the evenings, although she "might watch an old film on Saturday afternoon". She claims that her husband watches television more than her, which makes him prickle defensively. He admits that he might do so in the winter, but "in the summer I'd rather go out". He expands the point: "In the summer I go out mostly. I can't bear to watch ... if it's still light."

The man rather resentfully explains that the fact that his mother and daughter (who have rather different tastes to him) each have television sets in their own rooms doesn't prevent competition for the use of the main set in the living-room, because: "Everyone wants to watch this set. They're too lazy to go in their own rooms. A few years ago people used to say, 'I wish I had a car.' Now it's 'I'm not driving that – I don't like blue ones!' They're spoiled for choice!"

This man claims to have resisted getting the video recorder and states that they "only use it for three things a week". Later he distances himself from the machine even more. "I don't think ahead. See, a programme's normally gone before I think of recording. I just can't get into the sort of mechanics of getting up. It's still a mystery to me, that thing. In fact, I just don't know how to use it really. My daughter knows. I didn't know that you could record when the television's off till ten minutes ago when you told me."

This view of things is then later challenged by their daughter, as part of what seems like an established mode of expressing family tensions, through disputes around use of the television and video. The daughter claims that "he [her father] uses it most", to which her father rather crossly replies, "I only use it so she can watch my television and I watch what I've taped when she's gone to bed. That's the only reason I use it."

With regard to video hire, the man explains that "that's something she [the daughter] does more". On his part, this is largely because their local video shops do not cater for his tastes: "What there is to offer is appalling – there's four thousand to five thousand films and only about three you would want to watch. All the rest is *Kung Fu, Dirty Harry* ... I thought you could get things like *Oliver Twist* and Dickens but you can't get that."

Their video doesn't seem to be used to facilitate family viewing. The husband says later to his wife: "I don't think we've all actually sat down and watched a film together. You and I have, but I don't think our daughter watched it with us."

On the other hand, given that his wife and daughter have very different tastes from him they find the video a boon in so far that it means that he can sometimes be prevailed on to tape and watch later on his own the things that they don't like (history programmes, opera, etc.). "That is something the video is very useful for – because we can't stand it" (that is, *Chronicle*, one of the husband's favourite programmes).

The husband gives a very straightforward account of how power (and gender) relations in this family determine the outcome of conflicts over viewing choices: "Well, the biggest wins, and that's me. I'm the biggest." This contrasts strikingly with his wife's account of how her mother-in-law, in an equally classical feminine way deals with such conflicts: "Well, she likes *Dynasty*, in actual fact, she knows we can't stand it, so on a Saturday night – I mean, we do tend to sit and watch television if we're not going out, and she will go up to her room knowing that we don't like it, and watch it on her set. That's fine."

The husband prefers to watch television in silence. But family life makes this a little difficult.

Interviewer: "When you watch it, do you actually tend to watch in silence or do you sort of carry on chatting?'

Man: "I like to watch in silence."

Woman: "There's not much chance, is there?"

Man: "It's difficult – the dog's barking and our daughter's screaming. I do like to watch in silence."

Woman: "That's why you tend not to actually watch things that you really want to watch until later, until the phone's stopped going."

Man: "That's right, I'd rather record things and play them much later when it's quiet, when she [their daughter] is in bed and Mum's gone and the dog's gone out. It does tend to be a very busy house. It's normally after about nine-thirty at night when you've actually calmed down and you can watch something. I get very irritated if someone comes in when I'm watching TV." This is a point confirmed later by his daughter, who complains, "We get, 'Shut up and don't fidget!'"

In terms of tastes for particular programme types this man fits into the standard pattern of my sample. His preference is for factual programmes. He says that he watches the news "almost every night. I like that *Question Time*. That's the sort of thing – news programmes, topical. I tend to watch the news every time it comes on, on the different sides." Beyond this, he likes historical programmes (which connects both with his hobby as a local historian and with his work as a dealer in antique furniture): "I like historical programmes – *Chronicle* is probably my favourite programme. We [he seems to mean "I"] tend to like that more sort of minority – Channel Four is pretty good. There ought to be a channel for completely historical things ... and opera. I like to watch it when everyone's out because no one else likes it."

This is one part of a larger pattern of leisure interests which also involves his extensive use of their local library: "I love the library. Our library is really good. I wish it were open Sundays. There's a section on local history. It's open till about 8pm." Beyond this, he used to be a performer of traditional music and has a considerable interest in non-popular music. "I'm into opera, well, classical music anyway or blues and jazz. On the TV and radio you get what they call folk music. Like the Spinners! I mean, that's like Boy George!"

Daughter: "What's wrong with Boy George?"

This interchange between father and daughter clearly catches a small slice of an ongoing dynamic in the family where the father defines himself as part of a cultured minority and scorns popular television and music, much to the annoyance of his daughter who identifies strongly with these things. Thus later when discussing *EastEnders*, the daughter justifies the programme, against her father's rejection of "popular culture" – which is part of his concern that he and his family should escape from his own working-class roots (despite his enthusiastic identification with certain portrayals of working-class culture on television).

Daughter: "I like *EastEnders*. They are making programmes and making money out of it. People watch it."

Father: "I'm not saying it's not popular."

Daughter: "Well then, stop moaning about it. Just because you don't like it you can't persuade everyone else that loads of people watch it and it makes you talk cockney."

Her father's views on popular television are perhaps best encapsulated in his earlier comment that the crucial point is that "You've got to discriminate, haven't you?" This is in the context of his wife's explanation that they, as a couple, "can't stand *Dynasty*", although her husband admits, with some embarrassment, that my mother likes it, and *Dallas*", (and in his view she clearly functions as a "bad influence" on his daughter in this respect). *Dallas* and *Dynasty* are contemptuously dismissed as "all the same programme". Interestingly, in this family the woman does not occupy the traditional feminine position as a soap opera fan. Indeed, she makes a point of distancing herself from that type of programme.

Woman: "There's a thing about Australian doctors which my mother-in-law watches. It's like a bad *Crossroads*."

Matters are not quite as simple as this, however. It is presumably her recent re-entry into the world of education as a mature student of law that most clearly signifies her departure from the classic feminine/housewife position. Her husband cannot resist teasing her about how recent this transition was.

Man: "You used to be a *Crossroads* fan."

Woman: "It's amusing, but..."

Man: "You got quite carried away with it, I can remember."

Woman: "It's a bit like that. You get hooked on it."

Of course, these things are not one way. Later, when her husband has been presenting himself as a lover of serious programmes and high culture, his wife returns the "tease" in kind, pointing out that he does like *The Two Ronnies* and *Minder*. This is a betrayal against which the husband defends himself anxiously – and aggressively – by pointing to his wife's weakness for sentimental programmes.

Man: "I'm not keen on that sort of programme."

Woman: "Well, it's on now."

Man: "Yes, I watch it, but – The thing I can't stand is the quiz programmes. *The Price Is Right* and the other thing is *This Is Your Wife* [sic]."

Woman: "*This Is Your Life*. We watched it last night."

Man: "[She] loves it if there's a nice cripple on – no arms, no legs!"

In terms of fiction, the husband's preferences are for *Minder*, *Only Fools and Horses*, *Cheers* and *Auf Wiedersehen Pet*. Of the latter he says enthusiatically, "It was really terrific. After a while the characters were fantastic. That's something that I wouldn't miss." He is also enthusiastic about *Hill Street Blues*: "There are three or four of my friends who like *Hill Street Blues*. If we are in, we will go and watch that."

Conversely, it is *EastEnders* for which he reserves the greatest scorn. It becomes clear that this is because portrayals of London working-class life on television come a bit close to the bone as far as he is concerned, especially any romanticisation or glorification of the culture, which is aborrent to him as one who has struggled hard to escape from it. "It might be amusing for people who weren't brought up in that sort of environment like I was. The background to me is synonymous with ignorance. A lot of people see it as the 'salt of the earth', you know, 'great characters'. I don't see it that way! 'Cause I was brought up in that environment. It really does play up to it – 'gorblimey' and they seem to think that's great. They might find it amusing. I don't. It's the attitudes that people portray on there – very sort of narrow-minded. I don't like it." By contrast, he has nothing but praise for *Only Fools and Horses*, which he feels gives a much more acceptable portrayal of the same environment and one with which he definitely identifies. "It's great. It portrays the same sort of characters as in *EastEnders*, but there's more depth to them, they've got a bit more – they're quite bright – although they haven't had the education, but they're quite clever people." As he later explains, the programme doesn't just provide a historical identification with his past, but also with his present work.

"With some of my friends we always talk about *Only Fools and Horses*. It's very true to life. It's like the people I deal with a lot of the time. I buy and sell furniture. Whoever wrote that must have known lots of dealers, because everything that's said is absolutely spot on. I know all those characters and we all say, 'Did you see such and such? Wasn't it like when Tom did this?' We would always refer to an actual instance. It was uncanny sometimes."

This very positive reaction to *Only Fools and Horses* is simply the other side of the coin from a strong dislike of American programming – as is implied in this man's explanation of his reason for disliking most "American things" (and his reason for liking one particular American documentary as an exception): "That was a very good film, for an American thing. It wasn't over-glamorised."

Family 8

The husband here is thirty-nine, his wife forty. They have a daughter aged sixteen and a son of twelve. Both husband and wife left school at fifteen. The husband is a self-employed carpenter/glazier running a successful small business. His wife is a helper in a local school. They own their pleasant, newly-furnished house, and have lived there for eighteen years (moving here from only one mile away). Their nearest relatives live in the same street. They have one colour television, two black and white sets, a video recorder and a home computer. They took one holiday in the last twelve months. The man is involved in a number of sports (he is a member of a badminton club and also does weight-training) while his wife has "settled" for a more comfortably domestic middle age. The husband is a Conservative voter, his wife a Liberal supporter.

For this family, as contrasted with the others in this category, the television is a fairly constant fact of life. Rather than being restricted to late evening viewing, as the wife explains: "It's on all the while – unless we've got company. We switch it off then, but normally it's on. Normally if somebody comes round, we turn if off. We don't have the television on. We tend to play records then, don't we? Background music, you know."

This is a fairly well-established convention of their family life, which is matched by another one – their Sunday evening ritual of family viewing. This is the only time they will all sit and watch (either a video or broadcast television) together. Woman: Sunday evenings, we'll tape a film and then we'll probably watch that instead, you know. Sunday evenings, there's nearly always – we're all here from about seven-fifteen on, and we watch the television then, together."

However, the weekday routine is simply that the set will be on, pretty much regardless of whether anyone is watching it. If anyone is watching it is unlikely to be the whole family. It is simply that the set is on. This is something which the wife basically attributes to their children's (and in particular their son's) habits. "Normally it's on. I mean the children – not so much my daughter, but my son – especially in school holidays, he comes downstairs and it goes straight on. I think it's just habit really – first thing in the morning. Well, you see, again, directly when my son comes in from school the television goes on. So it's on really from say 4pm, except when they're doing homework, but then he'll probably just go off to do his homework and leave it on. But, you know, that's the first thing that goes on, isn't it?"

In terms of channel loyalties the wife explains that "We don't watch BBC, apart from if there's a good film on. It's mainly ITV. We don't watch a lot of BBC programmes." However it is not clear that this is so much a statement of empirical fact as a statement about their images of what types of programmes are predominantly associated in their minds with the various channels. Therefore the statement probably means that they only watch things on BBC which are like "ITV programmes".

In terms of gender and power relations, matters are quite clear. While the husband has ultimate power in any programme choice conflict, he at least is quite self-conscious about it: "We normally tape one side and watch what I want to watch!" Equally clearly, possession of the automatic control device is clearly a male prerogative.

Woman (to son): "You're the keeper of the control."

Son: "Either me or Dad has it. I have it mostly."

In a sense, this power balance, with masculine domination of the set, is not even experienced as a problem by the wife, because of her much more disinterested attitude to television as a whole (although this could be an attitude adopted defensively in the face of a situation she is unable to change). As she explains, she doesn't usually even bother to look at what is on the television in the schedules. She has a much more take-it-or-leave it attitude towards television and is quite happy to fit in with the desires and suggestions of the rest of the family – predominantly of her husband and son.

Wife: "I think I'm the only one that doesn't tend to check the television programmes. I tend to go, 'Oh, what's this?' I have my favourites, obviously, but I usually only watch if someone says, 'There's a good film on tonight,' you know. I don't think about it an awful lot, do I? If I miss something, I miss it." One of the few times when she speaks of putting the television on herself is when she is cooking. "I do tend to put it on when I come in from work on Friday, in the kitchen. It's a little radio-television. I enjoy anything then. I'm cooking, but I do have it on then." This provides yet another instance of women deriving most pleasure from television when watching while performing some domestic task, not least because their viewing is then free of guilt.

The wife's overall disengagement from television is compounded by her alienation from their video machine (like most of the women in my sample, she claims no understanding of machinery and thus doesn't trust herself to operate the video). These factors work together to reinforce each other. "If I want something, like if I - like when *Only Fools and Horses* used to be on a Thursday - I used to be washing my hair that time. Somebody'd tape it for me. Otherwise I don't think I've ever really... No, it's things like that *Fools and Horses*, *Summer Wine* that I used to really like to watch - but anything else - you know, if I was doing something else, well, tough, you know - I miss it."

In terms of gender and viewing style, this couple fit the pattern established in most of the other families in my sample. He prefers to watch in silence, she characteristically chats while watching - especially when her husband is watching things she isn't interested in, such as science programmes, or news and current affairs, or adventure films.

Woman (guiltily): 'I suppose we do chat a little bit. Isn't it awful, when you sit and think. We tend to chat, we don't sit in complete silence. We chat through everything, don't we? We don't rabbit the whole time - just most of it."

Man: "Science programmes, you're not always interested in. I like to listen to them, but - "

Woman: "We tend to talk," [that is to say, woman and daughter].

Man: "I try to listen to it. There might be a film on that they're not particularly interested in and I'll try and listen to it - then I'll miss half of it."

The wife's cultural tastes are very traditional, as she explains: "Like Sunday lunchtimes - years ago - you used to have *Round the Horn*. I used to have that. I always get *Woman's Own*. I like love stories. The last one I read was *Flora* - it was a lovely romantic story, it was great. I tend to read things like that. I change books with my sister-in-law - like the *Thorn Birds*."

Interestingly, despite her basically "distracted" viewing style, there is a point at which she will switch to a much more attentive style of viewing - in relation to the one type of programme (romance) which appeals strongly to her. This provides the exception to the rule of take-it-or-leave-it viewing while chatting.

Woman: "We tend to talk about some of the *Bestsellers*. We used to like watching that *Thorn Birds* - that was a big thing, wasn't it? Then nobody spoke. We sat there and we watched - made sure the cup of coffee was ready made."

The family's teenage daughter (along with a number of other teenage girls in the sample) has a strong preference within the category of soap opera for *Brookside* (which she views as "realistic" and can identify with, and talks to her friends "down the stables" about) as against *Dallas* or *Dynasty* (which she dismisses as glossy and unrealistic, offering her no point of identification). "I like to watch *Brookside*. It's my favourite programme. I like to listen to it, but everybody else chats! I don't know why – it's just good – 'cause down the stables everyone else watches it. It's something to chat about when we go down there. I don't like *Dallas* and all that, it's – I think it's because it's not real, I suppose. It's because they're not English, I suppose. We just sit and watch it, and some of it's quite funny. We don't really watch *Dallas* or *Dynasty*. At least in *Brookside* they haven't all got swimming-pools in the back gardens and oil-fields and things like that. It's not so glamorous. It's more sort of down to earth – even if it is sort of pretend – you know that most of it isn't real, but it's more sort of down to earth than *Dallas*."

Her mother dislikes *Dallas* for a rather different reason – because of its continuing themes of domestic disorder and conflict. "It's just the way they act, isn't it? I mean, the women are always arguing with one another. No one seems to get on. I don't know how they manage to live with one another. They're always arguing – all the time, you know – it's like that every week, it's the same thing. They're never happy, are they? I don't know what it is. It just gets on your nerves."

As she explains in her comments on her preferences within the categories of drama and comedy, like her daughter she also prefers programmes (preferably featuring working-class characters set in London) which seem realistic and with which she can identify: "I like watching Dell Boy in *Fools and Horses* and *Minder* with Arthur, it's all – they are characters you can sort of relate to – you've probably met – you know somebody who may be like them. I don't know, they're so real somehow, they're, you know ..."

But she explains that the fundamental criterion for her is the presence or absence of violence and disorder (whether in fictional or real terms) within different programme types. This is why she expresses such a strong preference for comedy (*Only Fools and Horses*, *Cheers*, *Last of the Summer Wine*), because it doesn't confront her with either of the elements she dislikes. "A lot of it seems to be comedy that I like, 'cause if it's films I don't like violence very much. I quite like *Hill Street Blues*. It was *Sweeney* that I didn't like. Horror films I can't watch – I'm like that all the time."

Her preferences certainly have a strong consistency, across all programme types, which is produced by this basic criterion. This also colours her attitude to news programming, which she explains is too "depressing" – presumably because of the violence and disorder which is of course the staple diet of television news. "I find it really depressing. We'll watch the 6pm news maybe. That's about the only time we have it on."

This structure of preferences on her part does not of course simply inform her own viewing choices; it also affects her husband's ability to watch the kind of news and documentary material in which he is interested. "Well, I don't mind *Question Time*. I used when living alone to like watching that. I think that's pretty good for current thinking." To woman: "You're not really interested in that, are you? So a lot of them shows, I don't get to watch them." This at least demonstrates the ways in which the structure of masculine hegemony within the family is also limited at various points by the need to recognise the desires and concerns of feminine family members.

The husband's tastes in television fiction are quite up-market, and he demonstrates a preference both for more complex programme types (such as *Hill Street Blues*, for example) which utilise a mix of elements from different genres and for fairly subtle comedy (*Cheers*) alongside his more predictable preference for *Only Fools and Horses* (on the basis of its realism and his ability to identify with the characters in it).

"*Hill Street Blues* I like. If we're not in, I try and tape it. *Cheers* is pretty good. *Fools and Horses* - that's a real good programme - I make an effort to watch that. Like with *Hill Street Blues*, there's so much going on all the time, you go from one thing to the other. It's not all violence - there's a bit of comedy in it. Like those other police series, it's all just car chase. With *Hill Street Blues* it's not all the same. With *Fools and Horses* you can imagine someone like that, you know - you get people like that - it's sort of true. *Cheers*, it's dropping off a bit now, but it's still quite dry and witty. I try and watch it most times it's on."

When asked about which types of programmes he might talk about with friends or workmates he mentions the *Kenny Everett Show*. "We might talk about those comedy shows that are on, like *Kenny Everett* - or the do-it-yourself bloke - because being a carpenter..."

This man is a fairly keen badminton player. When asked about his interest in sport on television he displays the predictable masculine preference for "real" activity over watching television. Indeed despite being quite an active sportsman (badminton, weight-training) he has very little interest in sport on television: "I'd rather play it than watch it, so I don't particularly, if it's on, rush home and turn it on. If there's something else - like a film - I'd rather watch a film than that, unless it's something very special, like a cup final, or a big fight, or whatever."

With regard to the operation of the video recorder, the wife won't use it herself, but she will ask someone to operate it for her if she wants something recorded. Apart from her take-it-or-leave-it attitude to television as a whole, this is also quite simply because she has no confidence with "machines".

The main person to benefit directly from the video is their daughter, who is out horse-riding and working in the stables at weekends and thus would miss a lot of things without the video: "I don't see anything. I work on Sundays – that's where the video comes in handy."

Again, as in a number of the other families, while the wife had initially been uninterested in the idea of getting a video (usually it was the husband who was the prime mover in getting one), she had gradually come to see it as of great benefit in her capacity as parent, managing the needs of others in the household.

Woman: "I didn't see the point in getting it at first, not really. I think it was good afterwards. Like we used to say to my son Mark, 'You're not staying up that late,' and his friends'd call him a baby if he didn't see the programme. So we tape it and he can watch it the next day early in the morning."

The parents do make some use of the video themselves socially: "Sometimes we'll plan to go and get something out [that is, rent a video film] and watch it – like we wanted to see *The Bounty* again. One of our friends got that as well, so we went round to her house and watched that. We do that . . ." But, as in a number of other families, it is mainly their children who use the video socially with their friends.

Woman: "School holidays, their friends'll come round."

Their daughter gives a fascinating account of how the context of this kind of teenage social viewing transforms the nature of socially permissible responses to programme material: "If I'm sitting with my friends and it's scary, we can just have a good laugh about it. We saw *Phantasm* and it was horrible. But because there was about six of us sitting there, it was OK. If it had been just two of us, I wouldn't have watched it on my own. I went to my cousin's house once and he had all his mates there and we watched *The Flesh Eater*, and I couldn't sit there going 'Ugh,' 'cause they were all sitting there watching it, so I had to watch it and it was horrible, because I was the only girl there and I felt really embarrassed."

Family 11

The husband is thirty-four, his wife thirty-six; they have two daughters of three years and eight months. The husband left school at eighteen, his wife at sixteen. He is in quite a senior position as a recruitment manager in the Civil Service and his wife is a part-time secretary in a local college. They own their large house and have lived here for ten years, moving there from only two hundred yards away.

Their nearest relatives live elsewhere in London. They have one colour television and one black and white set and a video, and they took one holiday in the last twelve months. He is very much a cockney lad made good, whose humorous self-presentation as such is self-consciously undercut by his clearly articulated grasp of both managerial and political issues. He is an active member of their local Labour Party, and his wife is also a Labour voter.

This couple are very committed to the idea that television viewing *should* be, above all, selective. The woman in particular feels guilty both about the kinds of things she watches and the amount she watches. "We watch far too much! Every evening, it's on when our daughter comes home from school until I go to work in the evenings. And then I would come back home and from 9pm it'll be selective viewing. It'll be something we've taped or something that we want to watch. But I have it on in the mornings – through my little girl, actually. She's started to put it on. I tend to sit and watch *Breakfast Time* stuff . . . something I vowed I'd never do. I was totally uninterested in it when it came on. Had my little girl not sort of switched it on, I would have never – it's on for most of the morning and it's on for *Play School*. Though I never, ever have it on in the afternoons."

Her husband expands the point in his comments about the off switch: "Saturday nights if we're in, we'll watch all evening – sometimes the programmes, sometimes a video. Other nights, I think we're both aware of the power of the on/off switch, and it's mainly off." As far as he is concerned, watching television is basically second-best to "real" activity. "If it's good weather, we're out in the garden, or visiting people." As he explains later, when his wife goes out to work and he is left with the kids, the set will go off. "I've got a book and a crossword lined up for when she goes out – rather than just watch TV."

The husband also explains the limitations on their viewing imposed by having young children, and his view of how they use their video – in distinction to what he knows of other couples with videos: "We very rarely watch after 11pm (because of having to get up early for the kids). The video has given us a lot more sleep. Yes, it's a toy, a good toy. We use it very much as a toy. We're not the sort of couple . . . I've known instances where they go out and get four films and they just sat there and seen eight hours of – we wouldn't do that. We use it selectively. We've not hired many films – about twenty in three years."

Interestingly, his wife also notes the significance of the ability to time-shift programmes in relation to the degree of attention they will give to something they've taped, as opposed to what just happens to be on broadcast television. "In the evening, when I come home and we sit down to actually watch something, it's more likely to be something we've taped." This is the main function of the video for them. The woman claims that "having the video has made us a lot more selective". They clearly use the video a lot, but strictly as a convenience for themselves, not as a basis of social occasions. The woman explains that it is "very rare" that they'd watch the video with guests, having tried it once and experienced that as a major social failure. "Very rare. We did it once – invited some people round. It's the only time we've had people come round and said, 'Let's all sit down and watch a film.' It was my birthday, last year. As a special treat I got *The French Lieutenant's Woman*, and everyone went to sleep they were so bored."

In terms of gender and viewing styles this couple fit into the overall pattern established in my research.

Woman: "I can't think of anything I'll totally watch. I don't just sit and watch. I'll probably sew – maybe knit. I'd very rarely just sit – that's just not me."

Man: "She tends to watch and do another activity at the same time."

Woman: "He's totally absorbed by it."

Man: "If I like it, I'm in there – in the action, feeling every blow, running every mile – especially something like live football – all sport, barring snooker. The Olympics was brilliant."

Like many of the other women in the sample, this woman too feels guilty about "just watching". She needs to feel that she is always doing more than that. She explains that she developed the habit of watching *Crossroads* while eating precisely for this reason: "Yes, I think it was when I was working full-time and I used to come home and that's the time when I'd be eating my meal. I actually like to watch something when I'm eating my meal, because it's like doing two things."

At the same time this woman's tangential relation to television as a whole also repeats the pattern identified by many of the other families whereby her lack of interest also means that she more readily cedes power to her husband in any conflict over programme choice. "It really is a question of, if there's something he wants to watch, I don't mind. I'm not really that interested."

This couple's preferences in terms of channel loyalties are also standard in this sample, the woman preferring ITV, the man BBC.

Woman: "Oh yes, ITV. Channel Four is coming into its own more now, but it's habit – you know, old habits die hard – you tended to watch on ITV, so you think that'll be more likely to be what you want to watch. It's certainly for me, anyway. I would probably look at

ITV first – I'm sure I do. It's not conscious but on reflection I'm sure I do."

Interestingly, her husband denies that they mainly watch ITV, quoting examples of programmes "they" watch (sports programmes, *Question Time*) which are on BBC. Unfortunately for his argument these turn out to be the programmes that he watches alone rather than with his wife.

Their tastes in terms of programme types are also typical. The woman refers principally to fictional programmes (in particular, *Crossroads* and *Dynasty*), her husband to factual programming: "I like sport, debate, research programmes such as *QED*, *TV Eye*, *Panorama*, *World in Action* – and nature programmes. It has to be a subject I'm interested in – *Time Watch*, *Survival*."

Here structures of class and gender overlap to give (on both counts) lower status to the programmes the woman likes – and from which the man is anxious to distance himself – and his image of them as a couple.

Man: "*Coronation Street* – no. We're not into that sort of repetitive television."

Woman: "You sound like a real snob."

Man: "I'm very snobby about some things. Sorry. *Crossroads* I tape for her."

Woman (guiltily): "Habit, I'm sure it is . . . pure habit. Because if I don't see it, it doesn't really bother me at all."

His wife's liking for "that kind of television" is a source of mild embarrassment to her husband, who teases her when she shame-facedly admits: "Yes, I watch things like *Crossroads*."

Man: "She's into *Blockbusters*!"

Woman: "Things like *Thorn Birds* – especially if I've read it."

Man: "Yes, we've had the lot. We've had *From Here to Eternity*, *Lace*, *Thorn Birds*, that one with Robert Mitchum – *Winds of War* – every – "

Woman: "I never watched *Winds of War*."

Man: "Yes you did! You see they all merge into one in the end – it's just one big epic."

Against this type of programme, the husband defines himself as a fan of something much more "highbrow" – Channel Four's *Hill Street Blues*. "*Hill Street Blues*. Now that's *real* television – it's got a lot of credibility – with the sub-plots. It's a hell of a good cast – they're small parts, lots of them, but they're real. Yes, we never miss an episode." Moreover his tastes in this respect are shared by his men friends, and *Hill Street Blues* is the one programme which he will admit to talking about on the basis of a genuine interest – in a way reminiscent of that in which many of the women in the sample say that they discuss soap opera with their women friends: "With my friends it's sort of things like should Renko marry or should Furrillo go back on the drink? Things like that – we'll debate that sort of thing."

While this man also explains that he will often use a discussion of television material in his professional capacity as a manager, in these cases it is a much more disengaged discussion which he will be entering into: "It's the telly as the first sort of gambit of establishing rapport, if you like, of setting the tone of the day. It's always a very good common denominator. 'What did you see on the telly last night?' It's always a gambit, isn't it, the telly? We do tend to use TV as a common denominator – almost with anybody. We feel safe with the telly, don't we? It's not like saying, 'Did you go to a political meeting last night?' You'd be using it as a topic, rather than you actually want to discuss what's on."

This man has a clear awareness of the varied potential uses of the medium – and of the potential of wilful misreadings of television: "If you're trapped into watching it, by circumstances, you can say, 'I'd rather read a book,' or you can try and absorb the story line and use it – as a store of misinformation and jokes." He is clear about what kinds of material might be "used" in this way (because it is of little interest to him in any other respect): "American rubbish – *Starsky and Hutch*, *Dallas*, *Dynasty*, *Street Hawk*. I can't stand those." This dismissal of "American rubbish" is the other side of the coin of what he really likes and identifies with – material set firmly in the area of London with which he identifies himself, and in particular *It's Only Fools and Horses*, which captures this situation best, in his opinion. "*Fools and Horses* – you're taking me back to my roots there. Well, Peckham, Bermondsey, Southwark, that's where I come from. And what I used to hate is actors trying to assume regionalised accents – right? And that's why I refuse to watch these like *EastEnders* or Jim Davidson. But when Dell Boy and Rodney get in front of that camera I don't mind if they're not cockneys, because it's beautiful, they've got the vernacular – they know what a cockney street character would say, it's come across very well... I mean, all right, forgetting censorship for a minute, you can't make it credible unless you swear – because "bloodies" are part of the cockney's vocabulary and Dell actually says 'plonker'. To a cockney they all know that means – but people watching it on BBC1, perhaps they don't. But it's really good. It's beautiful."

Family 16

The husband is fifty-two, his wife forty-six; they have a daughter of eleven and sons of nine and six. The husband left school at fourteen, his wife at nineteen. He is a self-employed (and successful) master builder and works very long hours to provide the financial support for their quite affluent life-style. His wife is a part-time secretary in a local school. They own a large house (which the man has clearly worked extensively on to modernise it to a very high standard) in a pleasant and leafy street, and they have lived here for eight years. Their nearest relatives live elsewhere in London. They have one colour television set with teletext and a video, and they took one holiday in the last year. The husband is a man who has worked hard for his own success, from a very working-class background, whereas his wife clearly comes from a rather better educated, middle-class background. He is an enthusiastic fisherman and a Conservative voter. His wife wavers between sympathies for the Conservative and Liberal Parties.

This relatively affluent family share many of the traits of the other families in this category, notably a tendency to restrict viewing to the late evenings (after about 9pm) on weekdays, and a definite commitment to "selective viewing" within that period.

In terms of gender/power relations this couple achieve quite a fine balance. Again it is the husband who uses the automatic control device rather than his wife.

Woman: "Yes. *He* uses it – the remote control."

Man: "Oh yes, quite a bit. I think, Oh I'll just see what's on the other side."

However, it is the wife who is the prime source of knowledge of the schedules and the husband clearly takes his cue from her suggestions.

Man: "Oh yes, I say to her, 'What's on the television?' of a night. If there is something worth watching, then I will make a point of watching."

Early in the interview the wife explains that they don't watch *Coronation Street* and similar programmes, first of all because she does not like soap opera but more fundamentally because "they're on at the wrong time of the evening and we tend to watch later." This point she repeats later, in relation to *Crossroads*; "It's the wrong time of the evening. The children are out and have to be fetched." Thus her not watching these programmes is not explained by one single cause. It is precisely an "overdetermined" form of causality (where more than one factor is in play) that is operative.

Her husband, who runs his own building firm, explains that it's mainly at weekends that he can watch, because he gets in so late from work during the week. "By the time we've had a meal it is usually after 9pm." Their viewing is clearly restricted on the whole, until after that time.

Of course, with their children, it is a different story: Woman: "The children switch it on when they come home, but when the weather gets warmer they are more in the garden. They are not so bothered with television." This is clearly an attitude which their parents are anxious to sustain. Later their father explains that he is actually worried about their children's tendency to view indiscriminately: "Well, the girl's at school now and this year's going to be – homework. So she's got to knuckle down and homework will come first and television afterwards. So we try to stop them getting square eyes by watching too much. I mean, the girl will watch television just for the sake of watching it. All right, educational programmes we don't mind them watching, you see, but sometimes if there's a programme on and it goes on rather late, they'll just sit there!"

The idea of "just sitting there" and watching television in this way is clearly abhorrent to this man, who says of himself, with some pride, "I don't sit for hours watching TV" and clearly feels some guilt about the extent to which he spends time watching television at all. This concern with the "rational" use of time is clearly not unrelated to his work life, as a self-employed man, where time is money in a very direct sense. This description of this mode of discriminatory viewing is clear. "I flick it on and have a look and if I don't like the programme I will turn it off and spend my time on something better. Unless there is a good film on or possibly certain types of plays and sport."

As he explains, his attitude is partly circumscribed by the demands of his work, but it is also a matter of principle to him – he feels strongly both that time shouldn't be wasted and that many television programmes are "a waste of time". "I can never say what time I'll be home. If there is something on, maybe at the weekend, if there is something on, I'll watch then, possibly Saturday evening and Sunday. In the rest of the week if there is a bit of sport or boxing maybe – but I don't really get down to watch much television."

Woman: "You don't watch much, do you? I watch if there is something good. I won't switch it on if there is nothing I'm interested in."

Man: "Quite frankly, a lot of the programmes they put on now are rubbish. They are not worth watching."

The woman differs from most in my sample in her dislike of soap opera. She does not watch *Coronation Street* or *Crossroads* – this is both a question of taste and of timing: "I usually watch in the evening. Ten o'clock news, television serials – not these soap ones. Like those Indian serials [*Jewel in the Crown*, etc.], all those big sagas. I like watching sport, not so much snooker except the final, but I like watching tennis. My boy always watches that David Attenborough one, *Life on Earth*. But we never watch these soap operas like *Dynasty* or *Dallas*. They get boring, and go on and on – like *Coronation Street*." As for *Dallas* and *Dynasty*: "They go on too long, and you find after a while it is nearly the same thing in each episode. Kenny Roger's *The Gambler* was a good programme, just for three nights, something like that, two or three nights is good, but the others, where they go on for years and years, you get enough around here . . . in this neighbourhood. You don't have to watch the TV to see those sort of things." She comments slightly ruefully that *Brookside* is something that appeals to her daughter (like many of the teenage girls in the sample) – "she would watch that more". Her own identification is quite strongly with up-market drama series, which is about the only form of television which she claims to talk about to other people: "Mums at school will say, 'Have you seen any good videos?' And *Jewel in the Crown*, yes, I would talk about that when I'm watching the big epics, big serials. I would talk about those."

In terms of the relationship between gender and viewing tastes established among most of my sample, this couple fit broadly within the terms of that divide – although, as becomes clear later, he does like some fairly up-market fiction series, and she does watch some news and current affairs programming. None the less the basic terms of the equation between masculinity and fact, and between femininity and fiction hold good, as evidenced in the husband's summary dismissal of "serials": "A lot of the programmes she watches, I won't watch. She watches serials. I won't."

Woman: "Oh, I watch a few serials he won't watch. I'm watching Peter Barkworth in *A late Start*, and *Mapp and Lucia*."

Later, as her husband expounds his taste for programmes on the border-line between current affairs and the chat-show format, the wife notes her enjoyment of their daytime equivalents:

Man: "We used to watch *Whicker's World* – that was a good programme – and *Terry Wogan* sometimes and Esther Rantzen I used to watch sometimes. Quite often *News at Ten*."

Woman: "If I'm in at lunch time I sometimes watch *Pebble Mill* or bits of it. I think I've watched *Sarah Kennedy* – one was very good. I just turned it on. I didn't realise that was on and I sort of sat and watched it."

However, notwithstanding this partial overlap of tastes, their primary tastes are quite different and the husband's enjoyment of some fictional programmes is secondary to his main interests: "The only thing for me, if we get down to it, is *Sportsnight*."

Woman: "I was watching that *Scott of the Antarctic* and Peter Barkworth. If I get time I'll sit down and watch a part of *Widows* or *Minder*. I watch *Quincy* sometimes."

Man: "Oh yes, and the *Lou Grant* one, and *Hill Street Blues*."

Returning later to his favourite programmes, he once again points to factual programming as his "real" preference: "I'll tell you what was an interesting programme – *Q.E.D.*. I've watched some of those and I watched one the other week where they found the bog man – that was very, very good. *World in Action* has good topics sometimes. As I say, I like sports programmes, any programme that's pertaining to a sport, live events. There are comedy shows I like. I watch a film if there's one on, or a decent play and generally topical things – the *World About Us*."

As far as this man is concerned, watching television is a clear "second-best" to "real" activity – especially his first love, fishing: "I like fishing, and I don't care what's on if I'm going fishing. I'm not worried what's on the telly."

However, this is not the end of the matter. His real concern in his prime leisure activity – also shapes his viewing choices when he has no better option than to watch television: Man: "Well, if there was a programme on that dealt with fishing, I would try my best to have a look at it, because, as I say, I like fishing. And when I go, I'm not worried what's on. Not so long ago they had one about people who were training to be sub-mariners. I like that, sort of real life. I like watching that sort of thing. I used to sit down and watch that, and *The Sailor* we watched, that was good. And I used to watch this really good German submarine thing...*The Boat* – anything like that, that's pertaining to real life, they're always worthwhile watching."

Here we see not only a coherence between overall leisure interests and viewing patterns, but also the more fundamentally and characteristically masculine preference for "the real" (in general) in terms of television programmes – whether they are news, current affairs, sport, crucially, as he puts it, "pertaining to real life" and therefore "worthwhile watching". Interestingly, this coherence is also visible in his preferences within the range of fictional programmes. Here it is the realism of the series to which he refers (in relation to his own work experience) that is the key factor in his selecting *Auf Wiedersehen Pet* for mention.

Man: "*Auf Wiedersehen Pet* – it's fantastic. I work in the building industry and it's typical of what goes on on a building site. I'd really like to see another series. It's a terrific bunch of characters." One of his other favourite programmes is *Hill Street Blues*, and again his explanation of this preference is in terms of realism – even though in this case this realism is not judged directly against his own personal experience. In the end the crucial point is that it is, in his view, "true to life". "Yes, it's a good series. That is, if you can understand the talk. But it's very good, it's well done, it's a good programme. Typical – you can imagine a police station and everybody screaming and shouting. It's more true to life. It's typical of what's happening in a busy police station where every five minutes the phone's ringing and another crime's been committed or somebody's been shot or something like that. It's very good. I like it."

His preference for this kind of relatively "serious" drama is also expressed in his basic channel loyalties (which are more a matter of his "images" of the different channels than empirical statements of fact), expressed as they are in terms of the image of BBC and Channel Four as presenting "intelligent" programmes, as opposed to his image of ITV, which is equated with the quiz programmes he dislikes so vehemently: "Perhaps BBC I watch a bit more – though Channel Four is beginning to get a better sort of programme."

In talking of what he doesn't like, we return to his central concern – the notion that a lot of television is a "waste of time": "To me what is a waste of time is all these quiz games. It's an insult to my intelligence – to expect me to watch pitiful women standing up screaming because they go up to London and answer a few questions. It is degrading to your mentality to think you can sit and watch that."

Interestingly, matters are quite different when he talks about comedy and light entertainment, where this man's tastes are unashamedly lowbrow, slightly to his wife's embarrassment.

Man: "I like Ray Moore and the Big Band Sound – things like that. *The Two Ronnies* – that's a fantastic programme, and of course the *Morecambe and Wise Show* used to be good. *The Benny Hill Show* – his are always good. Dick Emery, he used to be good. Ronnie Corbett, Cannon and Ball."

Wife: "I wouldn't sit down and watch those."

Television and gender

The interviews identified the following major themes, which recur across the interviews with the different families, where I can point to a reasonable degree of consistency of response. Clearly, the one structural principle working across all the families interviewed is that of gender. These interviews raise important questions about the effects of gender in terms of:

power and control over programme choice;
viewing style;
planned and unplanned viewing;
amounts of viewing;
television-related talk;
use of video;
"solo" viewing and guilty pleasures;
programme type preference;
channel preference;
national versus local news programming;
comedy preferences.

Before going on to detail my findings under these particular headings I would first like to make some general points about the significance of the empirical differences which my research revealed between the viewing habits of the men and women in the sample. As will be seen below, the men and women offer clearly contrasting accounts of their viewing habits – in terms of their differential power to choose what they view, how much they view, their viewing styles and their choice of particular viewing material. However, I am not suggesting that these empirical differences are attributes of their essential biological characteristics as men and women. Rather, I am trying to argue that these differences are the effects of the particular social roles that these men and women occupy within the home. Moreover, as I have indicated, this sample primarily consists of lower middle-class and working-class nuclear families (all of whom are white) and I am not suggesting that the particular pattern of gender relations within the home found here (with all the consequences which that pattern has for viewing behaviour) would necessarily be replicated either in nuclear families from a different class or ethnic background, or in households of different types with the same class and ethnic backgrounds. Rather, it is always a case of how gender relations interact with, and are formed differently within, these different contexts.

However, aside from these qualifications, there is one fundamental point which needs to be made concerning the basically different positioning of men and women within the domestic sphere. It should be noted that in the earlier chapters of this book there was much emphasis on the fact that this research project was concerned with television viewing in its domestic context. The essential point here is that the dominant model of gender relations within this society (and certainly within that sub-section of it represented in my sample) is one in which the home is primarily defined for men as a site of leisure – in distinction to the "industrial time" of their employment outside the home – while the home is primarily defined for women as a sphere of work (whether or not they also work outside the home). This simply means that in investigating television viewing in the home one is by definition investigating something which men are better placed to do wholeheartedly, and which women seem only to be able to do distractedly and guiltily, because of their continuing sense of their domestic responsibilities. Moreover, this differential positioning is given a greater significance as the home becomes increasingly defined as the "proper" sphere of leisure, with the decline of public forms of entertainment and the growth of home-based leisure technologies such as video, etc.

These points are well illustrated in research by Ann Gray into women's viewing and the use of video in the home. Gray argues that many women do not really consider themselves as having any specific leisure time at all in the home and would feel too uncomfortably guilty to "just" sit and watch television when there always are domestic tasks to be attended to.[1]

When considering the empirical findings summarised below, care must be taken to hold in view this structuring of the domestic environment by gender relations as the backdrop against which these particular patterns of viewing behaviour have developed. Otherwise we risk seeing this pattern as somehow the direct result of "essential" or biological characteristics of men and women *per se*. As Charlotte Brunsdon has put it, commenting on research in this area we could

"mistakenly... differentiate a male – fixed, controlling, uninterruptible – gaze, and a female – distracted, obscured, already busy – manner of watching television. There is some empirical truth in these characterisations, but to take this empirical truth for explanation leads to a theoretical short circuit... Television is a domestic medium – and indeed the male/female differentiation above is very close to the way in which cinema and television have themselves been differentiated. Cinema, the audiovisual medium of the public sphere [demands] the masculine gaze, while the domestic (feminine) medium is much less demanding, needing only an intermittent glance. This, given the empirical evidence ... offers us an image of male viewers trying to masculinise the domestic sphere. This way of watching television, however, seems not so much a masculine mode, but a mode of power. Current arrangements between men and women make it likely that it is men who will occupy this position in the home."[2]

From this perspective we can then see the empirical differences between the accounts of their viewing behaviour offered by the men and women in this sample as generated within this structure of domestic power relations.

Power and control over programme choice

Masculine power is evident in a number of the families as the ultimate determinant on occasions of conflict over viewing choices ("we discuss what we all want to watch and the biggest wins. That's me. I'm the biggest", Man, Family 4). More crudely, it is even more apparent in the case of those families who have an automatic control device. None of the women in any of the families use the automatic control regularly. A number of them complain that their husbands use the channel control device obsessively, channel flicking across programmes when their wives are trying to watch something else. Characteristically, the control device is the symbolic possession of the father (or of the son, in the father's absence) which sits "on the arm of Daddy's chair" and is used almost exclusively by him. It is a highly visible symbol of condensed power relations (the descendant of the medieval mace perhaps?). The research done by Peter Collett and Roger Lamb in which they videotaped a number of families watching television over an extended period shows this to comic effect on at least one occasion where the husband carries the control device about the house with him as he moves from the living-room to the kitchen and then engages in a prolonged wrestling match with his wife and son simultaneously so as to prevent them from getting their hands on it.[3]

F2 Daughter: "Dad keeps both of the automatic controls – one on each side of his chair."

F3 Woman: "Well, I don't get much chance, because he sits there with the automatic control beside him and that's it . . . I get annoyed because I can be watching a programme and he's flicking channels to see if a programme on the other side is finished, so he can record something. So the television's flickering all the time, while he's flicking the timer. I just say, 'For goodness' sake, leave it alone.' I don't get the chance to use the control. I don't get near it."

F15 Woman: "No, not really. I don't get the chance to use the automatic control. I leave that down to him. It is aggravating, because I can be watching something and all of a sudden he turns it over to get the football result."

F9 Daughter: "The control's always next to dad's chair. It doesn't come away when Dad's here. It stays right there."

F9 Woman: "And that's what you do [her husband], isn't it? Flick, flick, flick – when they're in the middle of a sentence on the telly. He's always flicking it over."

F9 Man: "The remote control, oh yes, I use it all the time."

F9 Daughter: "Well, if you're in the middle of watching something, Dad's got a habit of flicking over the other side to see the result of the boxing."

F8 Woman (to Son): "You're the keeper of the control aren't you?"

F8 Son: "Either me or Dad has it. I have it mostly."

F16 Woman: "Yes, he uses it a lot . . . the remote control."

F16 Man: "Oh yes, quite a bit. I think, Oh I'll just see what's on the other side."

In most of these families, the power relations are fairly clear. The man in F8 helpfully explains their family's way of resolving conflicts over viewing preferences:

F8 Man: "We normally tape one side and watch what I want to watch."

Interestingly, the main exceptions to this overall pattern concern those families in which the man is unemployed while his wife is working. In these cases it is slightly more common for the man to be expected to be prepared to let other family members watch what they want to when it is broadcast, while videotaping what he would like to see, in order to watch that later at night or the following day – given that his timetable of commitments is more flexible than those of the working members of the family. Here we begin to see the way in which the position of power held by most of the men in the sample (and which their wives concede) is based not simply on the biological fact of being men but rather on a social definition of a masculinity of which employment (that is, the "breadwinner" role) is a necessary and constituent part. When that condition is not met, the pattern of power relations within the home can change noticeably.[4]

One further point needs to be made in this connection. It has to be remembered that this research is based on people's accounts of their behaviour, not on any form of direct observation of behaviour outside of the interview context itself. It is noteworthy that a number of the men show some anxiety to demonstrate that they are "the boss of the household" and their very anxiety around this issue perhaps betokens a sense that their domestic power is ultimately a fragile and somewhat insecure thing, rather than a fixed and permanent "possession" which they can always guarantee to hold with confidence. Hence perhaps the symbolic importance to them of physical possession of the channel control device.

Styles of viewing

One major finding is the consistency of the distinction between the characteristic ways in which men and women describe their viewing activity. Essentially the men state a clear preference for viewing attentively, in silence, without interruption "in order not to miss anything". Moreover, they display puzzlement at the way their wives and daughters watch television. This the women themselves describe as a fundamentally social activity, involving ongoing conversation, and usually the performance of at least one other domestic activity (ironing, etc.) at the same time. Indeed, many of the women feel that to just watch television without doing anything else at the same time would be an indefensible waste of time, given their sense of their domestic obligations. To watch in this way is something they rarely do, except occasionally, when alone or with other women friends, when they have managed to construct an "occasion" on which to watch their favourite programme, video or film. The women note that their husbands are always "on at them" to shut up. The men can't really understand how their wives can follow the programmes if they are doing something else at the same time.

F2 Man: "We don't talk. They talk a bit."

F2 Woman: "You keep saying sshh."

F2 Man: "I can't concentrate if there's anyone talking while I'm watching. But they can, they can watch and just talk at the same time. We just watch it – take it all in. If you talk, you've missed the bit that's really worth watching. We listen to every bit of it and if you talk you miss something that's important. My attitude is sort of go in the other room if you want to talk."

F5 Man: "It really amazes me that this lot [his wife and daughters] can talk and do things and still pick up what's going on. To my mind it's not very good if you can do that."

F5 Woman: "Because we have it on all the time it's like second nature. We watch, and chat at the same time."

F18 Woman: "I knit because I think I am wasting my time just watching. I know what's going on, so I only have to glance up. I always knit when I watch."

F15 Woman: "I can generally sit and read a book and watch a film at the same time and keep the gist of it. If it's a good film it doesn't bother me. I'm generally sewing or something like that."

F9 Man: "I like to watch it without aggravation. I'd rather watch on my own. If it's just something I want to watch, I like to watch everything with no talking at all."

F9 Woman: "Every now and again he says, 'Ssshhh shut up.' It's terrible. He comes in . . . from a pool match and he'll say, 'Shut up, please shut up!'"

F9 Man: "You can't watch anything in peace unless they're all out. Half the time they start an argument and then you've missed easily twenty minutes of it . . . usually the catchphrase which you've got to listen to to find out what's going to happen in the programme. Sometimes I just go upstairs. It's not worth watching."

F11 Woman: "I can't think of anything I'll totally watch. I don't just sit and watch. I'll probably sew – maybe knit. I very rarely just sit – that's just not me."

F11 Man: "She tends to watch and do another activity at the same time."

F11 Woman: "He is totally absorbed by it."

F11 Man: "If I like it, I am in there in the action, feeling every blow, running every mile – especially something like live football."

F8 Woman: "I suppose we do chat a little bit. We tend to chat. We don't sit in complete silence. We chat through everything, don't we?"

F8 Man: "I try to listen . . . and I'll try and listen . . . then I'll miss half of it."

F12 Woman: "There is always something else, like ironing. I can watch anything while I'm doing the ironing. I've always done the ironing and knitting and that . . . You just sit down and watch it, whereas you've got things to do, you know, and you can't keep watching television. You think, Oh my God, I should have done this or that."

F4 Man: "I like to watch in peace and quiet, but there's not much chance. I do like to watch in silence.'"
F4 Daughter: "All we get is 'Shut up and don't fidget'. That's what he says when he's watching."

F17 Man: "I like to sit and concentrate. You lose the atmosphere if the children are mucking about."
F17 Woman: "I do a bit of knitting, and crocheting. He gives a running commentary while I'm doing the dishes after dinner, or when I'm in the kitchen. I know what's going on on the television, when he's with the boys. I know what's going on by his running commentary."

Charlotte Brunsdon, commenting on this and other research in this area, provides a useful way of understanding the behaviour reported here. As she argues, it is not that the women have no desire ever to watch television attentively, but rather that their domestic position makes it almost impossible for them to do this unless all the other members of the household are "out of the way":

> "The social relations between men and women appear to work in such a way that although the men feel OK about imposing their choice of viewing on the whole of the family, the women do not. The women have developed all sorts of strategies to cope with television viewing that they don't particularly like... However, the women in general seem to find it almost impossible to switch into the silent communion with the television set that characterises so much male viewing. Revealingly, they often speak rather longingly of doing this, but it always turns out to require the physical absence of the rest of the family."[5]

Again we see that these distinctive viewing styles are not simply characteristics of men and women as such but, rather, characteristics of the domestic roles of masculinity and femininity. The comments about the physical conditions under which women feel able to view attentively are explored further in the section below on solo viewing.

Planned and unplanned viewing

It is the men, on the whole, who speak of checking through the paper (or the teletext) to plan their evening's viewing. Very few of the women seem to do this at all, except in terms of already knowing which evenings and times their favourite series are on and thus not needing to check the schedule. This is also an indication of a different attitude to viewing as a whole. Many of the women have a much more take-it-or-leave-it attitude, not caring much if they miss things (except for their favourite serials).

F7 Man: "Normally I look through the paper because you [his wife] tend to just put on ITV, but sometimes there is something good on the other channels, so I make a note – things like films and sport."

F14 Man: "I just read the paper to see – and we might say there's something good on about 7.30 or 8pm – and we might turn it on. Otherwise it stays off."

F14 Woman: "I don't read newspapers. If I know what's going to be on, I'll watch it. He tends to look in the paper. I don't actually look in the paper to see what's on."

One extreme example of this greater tendency for the men to plan their viewing in advance in this way is provided by the man in F3, who at points sounds almost like a classical utilitarian aiming to maximise his pleasure quotient (in terms both of viewing choices and calculations of programme time in relation to video tape availability, etc.):

F3 Man: "I've got it on tonight on BBC, because it's *Dallas* tonight and I do like *Dallas*, so we started to watch *EastEnders* . . . and then they put on *Emmerdale Farm* because I like that, and we record *EastEnders* – so we don't have to miss out. I normally see it on a Sunday anyway . . . I got it all worked out to tape. I don't mark it in the paper, but I register what's in there. Like tonight it's *Dallas* then at 9pm it's *Widows*, and then we've got *Brubaker* on till the news. So the tape's ready to play straight through . . . what's on at 7.30pm? Oh, *This Is Your Life* and *Coronation Street*. I think BBC is better to record because it doesn't have the adverts. *This Is Your Life* we'll record because it's only on for half an hour, whereas *Dallas* is on for an hour, so you only use half an hour of tape . . . Yeah, Tuesday if you're watching the other programme means you're going to have to cut it off halfway through. I don't bother, so I watch the news at 9pm . . . yes, because there's a film at 9pm on a Tuesday, so what I do, I record the film so I can watch *Miami Vice*, so I can watch the film later." Or, as he puts it elsewhere, "Evening times, I go through the paper, and I've got all my programmes sorted out."

Again, the exceptions to this tendency are again themselves systematic – it is the women in F13 and F16 (who both in fact occupy the traditionally "masculine" position in the family) who do take responsibility for planning their (and their families') viewing.

F13 Woman: "No, well, I jealously guard the newspaper because people read the programmes out to me and I can't get it into sequence, you know, how many of them are running, so I won't be separated from the paper. I am the programme controller... He doesn't know what the programmes are all about and I say, 'I think you might like this,' so we give it a go, and see if he likes it or not... Yes, I tell him what I've heard about it and whether he'd enjoy it."

F16 Man: "Oh yes, I say to her, 'What's on the television?' of a night. If there is something worth watching, then I will make a point of watching it."

Amounts of viewing

In a number of these families it is acknowledged by both partners that the husband watches television far more than his wife.

F12 Woman: "I always say he is a TV addict. He'd have it on all day long."

F17 Man: "I watch more than she does."

F9 Woman: "I don't like television. It's very rare... it's got to be something very good for me to want to see it. It bores me. He's the one that likes the TV. When he goes out it won't be on."

F9 Man: "I watch telly – quite a bit of the time. If I'm in I'll always have the telly on. The nights I stay in I do watch the television. If I come in from work I'll turn on the TV. It's more like a habit."

F9 Woman: "Whereas I'll put records on. It's got to be something really good for me to put the telly on... I'm hard to please, I think, over anything on the television."

The women, on the whole, display far less interest in television in general except for the particular soap operas, which they are following.

F8 Woman: "I don't think about television an awful lot. If I miss something, I miss it. I don't... if I was doing something else, well, you know – I miss it."

F 3 Woman: "I can do a crossword and forget it... I am happy with what I see. He watches them films after we've gone to bed."

F11 Woman: "It really is a question of if there's something he wants to watch, I don't mind. I'm just not really that interested."

It might be objected that my findings in this respect conflict with (and are therefore perhaps "invalidated" by) the common survey finding that women report more viewing hours than men. However, I would argue that this is to do with the fact that in most families women are simply at home more than men and are therefore "available" as viewers more than men. My point is that while women are there, in front of (or rather, to the side, or in earshot of) the set, their dominant viewing practice is much more "bitty" and much less attentive than that of men. This is partly because there are so few programmes on, apart from soap operas, which they really like, and partly because their sense of guilt about watching television while surrounded by their domestic obligations makes it hard for them to view attentively. Thus, while more women may be "available" to view television more of the time and their potential viewing hours, considered as a mere matter of quantity, may be greater than those for men, when we consider attentive viewing (the key issue for this research project) their reported viewing is lower than that of men's.

Television related talk

Women seem to show much less reluctance to "admit" that they talk about television to their friends and workmates. Very few men (see below for the exceptions) admit to doing this. It is as if they feel that to admit that they watch too much television (especially with the degree of involvement that would be implied by finding it important enough to talk about) would be to put their very masculinity in question (see the section on programme type preference below). The only standard exception is where the men are willing to admit that they talk about sport on television. All this is clearly related to the theme of gender and programme choice and the "masculinity/femininity" syllogism identified there. Some part of this is simply to do with the fact that femininity is a more expressive cultural mode than is masculinity. Thus even if women watch less, with less intent viewing styles, none the less they are inclined to talk about television *more* than men, despite the fact that the men watch more of it, more attentively.

F1 Woman: "Actually my mum and my sister don't watch *Dynasty* and I often tell them bits about it. If my sister watches it, she likes it. And I say to her, 'Did you watch it?' and she says no. But if there's something especially good on one night – you know, you might see your friends and say, 'Did you see so and so last night?' I occasionally miss *Dynasty*. I said to a friend, 'What happened?' and she's caught me up, but I tend to see most of the series. Marion used to keep me going, didn't she? Tell me what was happening and that."

F2 Man: "I might mention something on telly occasionally, but I really don't talk about it to anyone."

F5 Woman: "At work we constantly talk about *Dallas* and *Dynasty*. We run them down, pick out who we like and who we don't like. What we think should happen next. General chit-chat. I work with quite a few girls, so we have a good old chat... We do have some really interesting discussions about television [at work]. We haven't got much else in common, so we talk a lot about television."

F6 Woman: "I go round my mate's and she'll say, 'Did you watch *Coronation Street* last night? What about so and so?' And we'll sit there discussing it. I think most women and most young girls do. We always sit down and it's 'Do you think she's right last night, what she's done?' Or, 'I wouldn't have done that,' or 'Wasn't she a cow to him? Do you reckon he'll get... I wonder what he's going to do?' Then we sort of fantasise between us, then when I see her the next day she'll say, 'You were right,' or 'See, I told you so.'"

F16 Woman: "Mums at school will say, 'Have you seen any good videos?' And when *Jewel in the Crown* was on, yes, we'd talk about that. When I'm watching the big epics, the big serials, I would talk about those."

F8 Daughter: "I like to watch *Brookside*, it's my favourite programme ... 'cause down the stables everyone else watches it – it's something to chat about when we go down there..."

F17 Man: "If we do talk, it'll be about something like a news programme – something we didn't know anything about – something that's come up that's interesting."

F18 Woman: "I'll talk about things on telly to my friends. I do. I think it is women who talk about television more so than men. I work with an Indian girl and when *Jewel in the Crown* was on we used to talk about that, because she used to tell me what was different in India. *Gandhi* we had on video. She told me what it was like and why that was interesting. Other than that it's anything. She went to see *Passage to India* and she said it was good, but it was a bit like *Jewel in the Crown*."

F18 Man: "I won't talk about television at work unless there'd been something like boxing on. I wouldn't talk about *Coronation Street* or a joke on Benny Hill, so other than that, no."

There is one exception to this general pattern – in F10. In this case it is not so much that the woman is any less willing than most of the others in the sample to talk about television but simply that her programme tastes (BBC2 drama, etc.) are at odds with those of most of the women on the estate where she lives. However, in describing her own dilemma, and the way in which this disjunction of programme tastes functions to isolate her socially, she provides a very acute account of why most of the mothers on her estate do spend so much time talking about television.

F10 Woman: "Ninety-nine per cent of the women I know stay at home to look after their kids, so the only other thing you have to talk about is your housework, or the telly – because you don't go anywhere, you don't do anything. They are talking about what the child did the night before or they are talking about the telly – simply because they don't do anything else."

In the main, the only television material that the men will admit to talking about is sport. The only man who readily admits to talking to anyone about other types of television material is the man in F11, who is a Civil Service manager. Primarily he talks about television at work, quite self-consciously, as a managerial device, simply as a way of "opening up" conversations with his staff, so he can find out how they're getting on, "using it as a topic, rather than you actually wanting to discuss what was on TV", or "as the first sort of gambit for establishing rapport . . . it's always a very good common denominator – 'What did you see on the telly last night?' "

Interestingly, beyond this conscious use of television as a conversational device in his role at work this middle-class man, exceptionally in my sample, also admits to having the kind of conversations with his men friends about fictional television programmes which, on the whole, only the women in my sample are prepared to admit to doing. Thus, this man is a keen fan of *Hill Street Blues* and will readily discuss with his friends issues such as "Should Renko marry? Should Furillo go back on the drink?". Even if there is a conscious tone of self-mocking irony in his account of their discussions, most of the men will not admit to having conversations of this type with the friends (especially about fictional television) at all.

The issue of the differential tendency for women and men to talk about their television viewing is of considerable interest. It could be objected that, as my research is based only on respondents' accounts of their behaviour, the findings are unreliable in so far as respondents may have misrepresented their actual behaviour – especially when the accounts offered by my respondents seem to conflict with established survey findings. Thus in principle it could be argued that the claims many of the male respondents make about only watching "factual" television are a misrepresentation of their actual behaviour, based on their anxiety about admitting to watching fictional programmes. However, even if this were the case, it would remain a social fact of some interest that the male respondents felt this compulsion to misrepresent their actual behaviour in this particular way. Moreover, this very reluctance to talk about some of the programmes they may watch itself has important consequences. Even if it were the case that men and women in fact watched the same range of programmes (contrary to the accounts they gave me), the fact that the men are reluctant to talk about watching anything other than factual programmes or sport means that their viewing experience is profoundly different from that of the women in the sample. Given that meanings are made not simply in the moment of individual viewing, but also in the subsequent social processes of discussion and "digestion" of material viewed, the men's much greater reluctance to talk about (part of) their viewing will mean that their consumption of television material is of a quite different kind from that of their wives.

Technology – the use of the video machine

None of the wòmen operate the video recorder themselves to any great extent, relying on husband or children to work it for them. This is simply an effect of their cultural formation as "ignorant" and "disinterested" in relation to machinery in general, and is therefore an obvious point, but one with profound effects none the less. Videos, like automatic control panels, are the possessions of fathers and sons (and occasionally of teenage daughters whose education has made them more confident with machinery than their mothers).

F2 Woman: "There's been things I've wanted to watch and I didn't understand the video enough. She [the daughter] used to understand it more than us."

F3 Woman: "I'm happy with what I see, so I don't use the video much. I mean lots of the films he records I don't even watch. He watches them after we've gone to bed."

F6 Man: "I use it most – me and the boys more than anything – mostly to tape the racing, pool, programmes we can't watch when they [the women] are watching."

F6 Woman: "Usually as my son goes out he'll leave me a little list with the girls – not with me, because I wouldn't do it 'cause I don't understand it. Well, I haven't got the patience, and I'll say to the girls, 'Tape that for me.' Otherwise I don't, very rarely, tape it, no, I'll leave them to tape it, because well, I'm all fingers and thumbs. I'd probably touch the wrong key. That's why I won't touch it."

F8 Woman: "I don't think about it an awful lot, do I? If I miss something, I miss it. I don't, if I was doing something else, well, you know, I just miss it."

F9 Woman: "I can't use the video. I tried to tape *Widows* for him and I done it wrong. He went barmy. I don't know what went wrong . . . I always ask him to do it for me because I can't. I always do it wrong. I've never bothered with it."

It is worth noting that these findings have also received

provisional confirmation in the research that Ann Gray has conducted. Given the primary fact of their tangential relation to the video machine, a number of consequences seem to follow – for instance, that it is common for the woman to make little contribution to (and have little power over) decisions over hiring video tapes; that it is rare for the woman actually to go into a video tape shop to hire tapes; that when the various members of the family all have their "own" blank tape on which to tape time-shifted material it is common for the woman to be the one to let the others 'tape over' something on her tape when theirs is full, etc.

As Gray puts it:

> "The relationship between the viewer and the television [or video machine]... is... a relationship which has to be struggled for, won or lost in the dynamic and often chaotic processes of family life... The VCR is... purchased or rented for use within these already existing structures of power and authority relations between household members, with gender being one of the most significant variations... women and men have differential access to technology in general and to domestic technology in particular... when a new piece of technology is purchased... [for example, the video] it is often already inscribed with gender expectations."[6]

Given that many women routinely operate sophisticated pieces of domestic technology, it is clearly these gender expectations, operating alongside, and framing, any particular difficulties the woman may experience with the specific technology of video that have to be understood as accounting for the alienation which most of the women in the sample express towards the video recorder.

Clearly there are other dimensions to the problem – from the possibility that the expressions of incompetence in relation to the video fall within the classic mode of dependent femininity which therefore "needs" masculine help, to the recognition, as Gray points out, that some women may have developed what she calls a "calculated ignorance" in relation to video, lest operating the video should become yet another of the domestic tasks expected of them.[7]

'Solo' viewing and guilty pleasures

A number of the women in the sample explain that their greatest pleasure is to be able to watch "a nice weepie", or their favourite serial, when the rest of the family aren't there. Only then do they feel free enough of their domestic responsibilities to "indulge" themselves in the kind of attentive viewing which their husbands engage in routinely. Here we enter the territory identified by Brodie and Stoneman (see note 19, Chapter 2), who found that mothers tended to maintain their role as "domestic manager" across programme types, as opposed to their husbands' tendency to abandon their manager/parent role when viewing material of particular interest to them. The point is expressed most clearly by the woman in F7 who explains that she particularly enjoys watching early morning television at the weekends – because, as these are the only occasions on which her husband and sons "sleep in", these are, by the same token, the only occasions when she can watch television attentively, without keeping half an eye on the needs of others.

Several of these women will arrange to view a video or film with other women friends during the afternoon. It is the classically feminine way of dealing with conflict – in this case over programme choice – by avoiding it, and "rescheduling" the programme (often with someone's help in relation to the video) to a point where it can be watched more pleasurably.

F5 Woman: "That's one thing we don't have on when he's here, we don't have the games programmes on because he hates them. If we women are here on our own – I love it. I think they're lovely ... If I'm here alone, I try to get something a bit mushy and then I sit here and have a cry, if I'm here on my own. It's not often, but I enjoy that."

F6 Woman: "If I get a good film on now, I'll tape it and keep it, especially if it's a weepie. I'll sit there and keep it for ages – especially in the afternoon, if there's no one here at all. If I'm tired, I'll put that on – especially in the winter – and it's nice then, 'cause you sit there and there's no one around ... We get those *Bestsellers* and put them together so you get the whole series together, especially if it's late at night. You're so tired – it's nice to watch the whole film together. We try and keep them, so of an afternoon, if you haven't got a lot to do, you can sit and watch them."

F7 Woman: "If he's taped something for me I either watch it early in the morning about 6am ... I'm always up early, so I come down and watch it very early about 6 or 6.30 Sunday morning. Now I've sat for an hour this afternoon and watched *Widows*. I like to catch up when no one's here – so I can catch up on what I've lost ... I love Saturday morning breakfast television. I'm on my own, because no one gets up till late. I come down and really enjoy that programme."

F15 Woman: "I get one of those love stories if he's not in."
F15 Man: "Yes, I don't want to sit through all that."
F15 Woman: "Yes, it's on his nights out. It doesn't happen very often."

F18 Woman: "I don't work Mondays and quite often my friends
will get a film and watch it up here. I've done that about three times. A
lot of my friends haven't got videos. They can't afford them. So it's
something special to them."

My findings in this respect are very clearly supported by Ann
Gray's research. Gray argues that her women respondents do have
definite preconceptions as to what constitutes a "film for men" as
against a "film for women", and on this basis she also develops a
typology of viewing contexts, for masculine and feminine viewing
(jointly and separately) along with a typology of types of films and
programmes "appropriate" to these different viewing contexts. Her
point is that quite different types of viewing material are felt to be
appropriate to the different viewing contexts of the whole family
together, male and female partners together, male alone and female
alone. Moreover, she argues that among her respondents, women will
only usually watch the kinds of material which they particularly like
when their partner is out of the house (at work or leisure), whereas the
men will often watch the material which they alone like while their
partner is there – she simply would busy herself around the house, or
sit without really watching.[8]

As Gray notes, women who are at home all day in fact have
obvious opportunities then to view alone, but for many of them
daytime television viewing is seen as a kind of "drug" to which they
feel, guiltily, that they could easily become addicted.

These comments bring us back to the issue already considered
concerning the sense in which the home simply is not a sphere of
leisure for women, and thus the ways in which their viewing is
constrained by guilt and obligation. However, beyond these
considerations there is another dimension which is perhaps even
more fundamental. As Ann Gray expresses it, summarising her
research in this area, "It is the most powerful member of the
household who defines this hierarchy of serious and silly, important
and trivial, which leaves women and their pleasures downgraded,
objects and subjects of fun and derision, having to consume [the films
and programmes they like] almost in secret."[9]

What is at issue here is the guilt that most of these women feel
about their own pleasures. They are, on the whole, prepared to
concede that the drama and soap opera they like is "silly" or "badly
acted" or inconsequential – that is, they accept the terms of a
masculine hegemony which defines their preferences as having a low
status. Having accepted these terms, they then find it hard to argue
for their preferences in a conflict (because, by definition, what their
husbands want to watch is more prestigious). They then deal with this
by watching their programmes, where possible, on their own, or only
with their women friends, and will fit such arrangements into the

crevices of their domestic timetables.

F3 Woman: "What I really like is typical American trash I suppose, but I love it ... All the American rubbish, really. And I love those Australian films. I think they're really good, those."

F17 Woman: "When the children go to bed he has the ultimate choice. I feel guilty if I push for what I want to see because he and the boys want to see the same thing, rather than what a mere woman would want to watch ... if there was a love film on, I'd be happy to see it and they wouldn't. It's like when you go to pick up a video, instead of getting a nice sloppy love story, I think I can't get that because of the others. I'd feel guilty watching it – because I think I'm getting my pleasure whilst the others aren't getting any pleasure, because they're not interested."

F10 Woman: "I would want to watch the sloppy films. He hates them. We just watched a film recently, in the afternoon ... The school bus is hit by a train and the woman loses her legs. I mean, I don't mind watching that, I know they're going to end up happy."

F14 Woman: "I read a lot of crap and all the scandal stuff – Harold Robbins and all that. The last one I really enjoyed, which I shouldn't have enjoyed, was *Lace*. I read it from cover to cover."

F9 Woman: "I like tear-jerkers, things that are really sad – more so than anything funny, because I don't like things funny. I like, really, tear-jerkers – something like *Thorn Birds*. Yes, I loved that one. It was really great."

Programme type preference

My respondents displayed a notable consistency in this area, whereby masculinity was primarily identified with a strong preference for "factual" programmes (news, current affairs, documentaries) and femininity identified with a preference for fictional programmes. The observation may be banal, but the strength of the consistency displayed here was remarkable, whenever respondents were asked about programme preferences, and especially when asked which programmes they would make a point of being in for, and viewing attentively.

F6 Man: "I like all documentaries ... I like watching stuff like that ... I can watch fiction but I am not a great lover of it."

F6 Woman: "He don't like a lot of serials."

F6 Man: "It's not my type of stuff. I do like the news, current affairs, all that type of stuff."

F6 Woman: "Me and the girls love our serials."
F6 Man: "I watch the news all the time, I like the news, current affairs and all that."
F6 Woman: "I don't like it so much."
F6 Man: "I watch the news every time, 5.40pm, 6pm, 9pm, 10pm, I try to watch."
F6 Woman: "I just watch the main news so I know what's going on. Once is enough. Then I'm not interested in it."

F4 Man: "I watch the news almost every night. I like that *Question Time*. That's the sort of thing. The news programmes, I tend to watch the news every time it comes on, on the different sides."

F7 Man: "The news - I always watch the 10pm news. I like documentaries."

F17 Woman: "Things I like least are things like *World in Action*, when it's more political. The *Money Programme* - there's too much talking. On the whole I don't bother too much with those kind of programmes. I don't like documentaries. I like something with a story, entertainment, variety."

F10 Man: "I must admit I prefer more factual television. I enjoy some of the *TV Eye* series. We have just watched the *Trojan War* - that was brilliant. I enjoy series like that - like *Life On Earth* - wildlife programmes, and *World in Action* ... I like to know about things because basically I am a working-class man and I like to know what is happening. I like to know what is happening to me personally ... I do enjoy watching factual programmes. I think I would much rather watch a factual programme."

F11 Man: "I like debate, research programmes such as *QED*, *TV Eye*, *Panorama*, *World in Action*, and nature programmes. It has to be a subject I am interested in - *Time Watch*, *Survival*."

Moreover the exceptions to this rule (where the wife prefers "factual programmes" etc.), are themselves systematic. This occurs only where the wife, by virtue of educational background, is in the dominant position in terms of cultural capital. One clear instance of this occurs in F13, where the man is a relatively uneducated council flat caretaker, but his wife is a highly literate woman who has recently started to attend college as a mature student. In this family the usual pattern of responses in my sample is reversed:

F13 Woman: "I like *Newsnight* very much. And *Question Time*. I might say to him, 'Look, this is about council estates in Wandsworth,' in which case ..." (that is, she thinks he ought to be interested).

F13 Man: "Yeah, then I'll watch it but if I'm sitting by myself, I'll watch *World in Action* if it's on, but I'd rather come in and watch a game of snooker than come in and watch *World in Action*."

F13 Woman: "It's the same with *Horizon*. I mean that was very interesting the other night. That was very interesting to me, but he would never have sat through the first five minutes."

As will be seen later, for the same reasons, this woman's responses are "out of line" with those of most women in the sample in relation to a number of the key themes identified. In this particular connection, it is not simply that she is more interested in factual programming than most of the women in the sample, but also that she is less interested in the kind of fictional programming that most of the women respondents are very keen on.

F13 Woman: "*Crossroads* doesn't appeal to me – it's terrible acting, and *EastEnders*, they make me want to scream, they seem so false. *Dallas* and *Dynasty* don't appeal to me, because he's too ridiculous that bloke J.R."

Interestingly, this very same refrain is taken up by the only other woman in the sample who is also now a mature student.

F4 Woman: "There's a thing about Australian doctors – it's like a bad *Crossroads*, but this is even worse."

One of the only two other women in the sample who had this negative view of soap opera is not a mature student, but did stay on at school to do A-levels (unlike most of the women interviewed). She is strongly influenced by her husband's political interests and activities and describes herself as "not a feminist, but..."

F10 Woman: "Before we were married, if *Dallas* was on I never went out... but now it has changed. I don't watch any of the soap operas at all. I'm not interested in them now."

What is interesting is that living on a council estate where most of the other women do not share her views of life, not watching this type of programming makes her social life very different, as it means she has one less "thing in common" to talk about to the other mothers on the estate.

F10 Woman: "The other mothers watch *Dallas* and *Dynasty* and all that. They can't understand why I don't watch *Crossroads*... Even though I'm a mum, I feel out of it because they don't watch what I do. They watch *Crossroads* and *EastEnders*, *Gems*, *The Practice*."

The only other woman to take this negative view of soap opera is the woman in F16. In this family, the wife is again more highly educated than her husband. In this woman's particular case it is prestigious television serials (*Jewel in the Crown*, etc.) which she prefers, "not these 'soapy' ones."

The argument also extends further. First, there is the refrain among the men that watching fiction in the way that their wives do is an improper and almost "irresponsible" activity, an indulgence in fantasy of which they disapprove (compare nineteenth-century views of novel-reading as a "feminising" activity). This is perhaps best expressed in the words of the couples in F1 and F6, where in both cases the husbands clearly disapprove of their wives' enjoyment of "fantasy" programmes.

F1 Woman: "That's what's nice about it [*Dynasty*]. It's a dream world, isn't it?"

F1 Man: "It's a fantasy world that everybody wants to live in, but that – no, I can't get on with that."

The husband in F6 takes the view that watching television in a way is an abrogation of civil responsibility.

F6 Man: "People get lost in TV. They fantasise in TV. It's taken over their lives... People today are coming into their front rooms, they shut their front door and that's it. They identify with that little world on the box."

F6 Woman: "To me, I think telly's real life."

F6 Man: "That's what I'm saying. Telly's taken over your life."

F6 Woman: "Well, I don't mind it taking over my life. It keeps me happy."

The depth of this man's feelings on this point are confirmed later in the interview when he is discussing his general leisure pursuits. He explains that he now regularly goes to the library in the afternoons, and comments that he "didn't realise the library was so good – I thought it was all just fiction". Clearly, for him, "good" and "fiction" are simply incompatible categories.

Secondly, the men's programme genre preference for factual programmes is also framed by a sense of guilt about the fact that watching television is a "second-best" choice in itself – in relation to a strong belief (not shared in the same way by the majority of the women) that watching television at all is "second-best" to "real" leisure activity:

F4 Man: "I'm not usually here. I watch it if there's nothing else to do, but I'd rather not... In the summer I'd rather go out. I can't bear to watch TV if it's still light."

F16 Man: "I like fishing. I don't care what's on if I'm going fishing. I'm not worried what's on the telly then."

F11 Man: "If it's good weather we're out in the garden or visiting people...I've got a book and a crossword lined up for when she goes out, rather than just watch television."

It is of note that these last quotes are all from families where the men have a particularly strong feeling that "just watching television" is not, on the whole, an acceptable activity. All of these three quotes come from men in category B. Their particular concern about not "wasting time" just "watching television" seems also to be related to their class position.

Moreover, when the interviews move to a discussion of the fictional programmes that the men do watch, consistency is maintained by their preference for a "realistic" situation comedy (a realism of social life) and a rejection of all forms of romance.

These responses seem to fit fairly readily into a kind of "syllogism" of masculine/feminine relationships to television:

Masculine	*Feminine*
Activity	Watching television
Fact programmes	Fiction programmes
Realist fiction	Romance

Again, it may be objected that my findings in this respect exaggerate the "real" differences between men's and women's viewing and underestimate the extent of "overlap" viewing as between men and women. Certainly my respondents offer a more sharply differentiated picture of men's and women's viewing than is ordinarily reported by survey work, which seems to show substantial numbers of men watching "fictional" programmes and equally substantial numbers of women watching "factual" programmes.

However, this apparent contradiction largely rests on the conflation of "viewing" with "viewing attentively and with enjoyment". If we use the first definition, then we can expect considerable degrees of overlap as between men's and women's "viewing". Once we use the second definition, the distinctions as between men's and women's preferred forms of viewing become much more marked. Moreover, even if this were not the case, and it could be demonstrated that my respondents had misrepresented their behaviour to me (offering classical masculine and feminine stereotypes which belied the complexity of their actual behaviour), it would remain as a social fact of considerable interest that these were the particular forms of misrepresentation which respondents felt constrained to offer of themselves – and these tendencies (for the men to be unable to admit to watching fiction) themselves have real effects in their social lives.

Further it could be objected that the fact that the respondents were interviewed *en famille* may have predisposed them to adopt stereotyped familial roles in the interviews which, if interviewed separately, they would not adhere to – thus again leading to a tendency towards misleading forms of classical gender stereotyping. However, this was precisely the point of interviewing respondents *en famille* – as it was their viewing *en famille* which was at issue, specifically in respect of the ways in which their familial roles interact with their roles as viewers. Accounts which respondents might give of their behaviour individually would precisely lack this dimension of family dynamics and role-playing.

More fundamentally, if one poses the issue as one in which "real" behaviour (as monitored by survey techniques) is counterposed to "unreliable" accounts offered by respondents, one runs the risk of remaining perpetually stuck at the level of external measurements of behaviour which offer no insight or understanding into what the observed behaviour means to the people concerned. Thus, monitoring techniques may seem to show that many women are "watching" factual television (as measured in terms of physical presence in front of the set) when, as far as they are concerned, they are in fact paying little or no attention to what is on the screen (not least because it is often a programme which they did not themselves choose to watch), as revealed by their comments when asked to give their own accounts of their viewing behaviour. Moreover, it is only through viewers' own accounts of why they are interested (or disinterested) in particular types of programmes that we can begin to get any sense of the criteria they employ in making the particular viewing choices they do.

Channel preferences

There is a tendency for men to claim to prefer BBC (and in some cases BBC2) rather than ITV, and for women to do the opposite. This has got some connection with the images of BBC as "educational" and ITV as "entertaining" – thus their preference is simply a homology with the programme genre preference explained above. These statements about "channel loyalty" are not to be interpreted as simple empirical statements – not least because the men, having stated a clear preference for BBC, will often then go on to enthuse about programmes which are in fact on ITV. However, these statements are still very significant, not only as indicators of the primary connotations associated with each channel. The point is that when the men then refer (unwittingly) to ITV programmes, they tend to be speaking of programmes which are in fact on ITV but which they would have expected to be on BBC in terms of their understanding of what type of programmes each channel primarily offers. The converse is true for many of the women, who state a clear preference for ITV and then often go on to enthuse about BBC programmes. Again, the BBC programmes they enthuse about tend to be the type of entertainment programmes which are primarily associated in their minds with ITV. Whilst this tendency is not consistent across all the families (for instance, in me, neither husband nor wife like BBC) the only cases of the cu.verse pattern (where the wife prefers BBC and the husband ITV) are those where the wife is, because of her educational background, in the "masculine" position.

F11 Woman: "Oh yes, I put ITV on. It's habit. Old habits die hard. You tend to watch ITV, so you think that'll be more likely to be what you want to watch. It certainly is for me anyway. I would probably look at ITV first – I'm sure I do. It's not conscious, but on reflection I'm sure I do."

F12 Woman: "ITV it's got to be for me. BBC will only go on for *Wogan* or something like that."
F12 Man: "I watch BBC2 quite a lot."

F5 Woman: "We're inclined to watch ITV more. He always puts on BBC2, no matter what's on."

F2 Man: "They all tend to watch ITV, but I think BBC2's got a lot of good things."

F15 Woman: "I think *Dallas* is the only regular programme we watch on BBC."

F8 Woman: "We don't watch BBC, apart from if there is a good film on. It's mainly ITV. We don't watch a lot of BBC programmes."

F16 Man: "Perhaps I watch BBC a bit more, though Channel Four is beginning to get a better sort of programme."

F1 Woman: "We tend to watch ITV more – well, I do."
F1 Man: "Sometimes I like the documentaries on BBC."
Once again, it is the interview in F13 which provides the clearest exception to this general pattern.

F13 Woman: "You notice the rubbish creeping on to the BBC now as well. *Cover Up*, it really belongs on ITV. *Minder*'s on ITV. That's quite amusing but I don't watch it very much."
F13 Man: "I don't go straight to Channel Four, but she does."
F13 Woman: "I don't think Channel Four talk down to you so much. I like things like *The Young Ones* and stuff like that, and the other channels are stuffy. I mean ITV is just soap, soap and more soap generally. And Channel Four seems to be more adult. Even the films they show are much better. That's the sort of thing you would see on Channel Four you wouldn't see anywhere else. If there's anything new on and I don't know what it is, then I'll give it a go if it's on Channel Four, but if it's on ITV I might well not try so hard to watch it."

National and local news programming

As has been noted, it is men and not women who tend to claim an interest in news programming. Interestingly, this pattern varies when we consider local news programmes, which a number of the women claim to like. In several cases they give very cogent reasons for this – as they don't understand what the "pound going up or down" is about, and as it has no experential bearing on their lives they're not interested in it. However, if there has been a crime (for instance, a rape) in their local area, they feel they need to know about it, both for their own sake and their children's sakes. This connects directly to their other expressed interest – in programmes like *Police Five*, or programmes warning of domestic dangers. In both these kinds of cases the programme material has a practical value to them in terms of their domestic responsibilities, and thus they will make a point of watching it. Conversely, they frequently see themselves as having no practical relation to the area of national and international politics presented in the main news and therefore don't watch it.

The clearest expression of this perspective is that offered by the woman in F9. As she explains, local news is of considerable interest to her.

F9 Woman: "Sometimes I like to watch the news if it's something that's gone on – like where that little boy's gone and what's happened to him. Otherwise I don't, not unless it's local only when there's something that's happened local." Whereas national news just "gets on her nerves". "I can't stand *World in Action* and *Panorama* and all that. It's wars all the time. You know, it gets on your nerves."

Her explanation of precisely why she doesn't view the national news is worth considering in some detail, as she explains her perfectly cogent reasons for not watching it. "What I read in the papers and listen to the news is enough for me. I don't want to know about the Chancellor somebody in Germany and all that. When I've seen it once I don't want to see it again. I hate seeing it again – because it's on at breakfast time, dinner time, and tea time, you know, the same news all day long. It bores me. What's going on in the world? I don't understand it all, so I don't like to listen to that. I watch – like those little kids – that gets to me, I want to know about it. Or if there's actually some crime in Wandsworth, like rapes and all the rest of it I want to read up on that, if they've been caught and locked away. As for like when the guy says the pound's gone up and the pound's gone down, I don't want to know about all that, 'cause I don't understand it. It's complete ignorance really. If I was to understand it all, I would probably get interested in it."

However, her response is merely the clearest expression of what is a very common pattern among most of the women in the sample.

F15 Woman: "*Reporting London* – more than anything in the news sort of line – we watch that. That's what's happening where we're living, in this city."

F2 Woman: "I like the one that's just after the main news for about five minutes – the *Thames News*. I've got something about that – I have to see it. Yes, it's only on for about five minutes. They tell you all the news, not as much as the other one, though they seem to tell you more, you know."

F3 Woman: "I like *Thames News*. I watch the six o'clock news and *Thames News* again on Friday with Michael Aspel."

F5: Woman: "ITV's best because that's *London Weekend*. It tells you what's going on in your area, so you're more interested."

F6 Woman: "I just watch the main news. So I know what's going on. Once is enough – then I'm not interested in it."

F14 Woman: "I'm not interested in news and all that stuff."

F8 Woman: "I find the news really depressing. We'll watch the 6pm news maybe. That's about the only time we have it on."

F3 Woman: "The only sort of film I would say to them to watch is an educational film, like if the police was to put one on warning children about strangers, then I'd make sure they'd watch it. I mean when Jimmy Saville used to have them on a Sunday – *Dangers in the Home*. I used to say to them, 'Now watch this because it's interesting. You can learn from them.' And that crime programme – *Crimewatch* – that's a good programme to watch because it gives you some idea of what to look out for…what the kids should look out for as well."

Comedy preferences

Quite simply, a significant number of the women interviewed display a strong dislike of "zany" comedy as a genre, and of *The Young Ones* in particular as an instance of this genre. On the other hand, their husbands, sons and teenage daughters all tend to like this type of comedy very much.

The main point here seems to be that for women for whom maintaining domestic order is their primary responsibility and concern, comedy of this kind is seen as something of an insult, in so far as it is premised on the notion that domestic disorder is funny. That is why, for instance, the woman in F9 dislikes it to the extent that she does. As the person in the household who is responsible when she comes in from work for getting everybody's socks clean and their food cooked, she does not find domestic disorder particularly amusing.

F1 Man: "We've got virtually the same taste apart from *The Young Ones*. I really like that. She hates it."

F3 Woman: "*The Young Ones* – I think that's a revolting programme. The things they come out with in it. But you [her daughter] think it's funny, you think it's really funny, don't you?"

F9 Woman: "*Kenny Everett* can't make me laugh. *Lenny Henry* doesn't make me laugh. You see, I don't find all that funny really... That's sickly [*The Young Ones*]. I think they're real sick. If that's on I do the washing, anything."

Again, the women who prove exceptions to this basic pattern are themselves systematic. It is the women who have moved out of their traditional, feminine position who do not conform to this basic pattern of response.

F14 Woman: "I like the *Young Ones* of course – though I don't actually turn the TV on to watch it." In her case her recent work experience at a drama college and her present involvement in setting up her own business go some part of the way towards explaining why she does not conform to the general pattern of feminine responses in this particular respect. Indeed her own prioritisation of her career over her domestic responsibilities is evident in the very layout of her own home: she is far less "houseproud" than most of the other women in the sample.

The other two women who are at odds with the standard pattern are the women from F10 and F13. As has already been mentioned, the woman in F10 has very different tastes in television programming from most of the other mothers that she knows. Their failure to grasp what it is that she likes about *The Young Ones* is simply the sharpest edge of this fundamental divide.

F10 Woman: "We were watching *The Young Ones* the other night. Oh, we did laugh. You see, none of the mums watch that. It's too intellectual for them. Now that has me in stitches, where they are locking him in the fridge and he falls out. And to them it's lost – it does not mean a thing. It must be on Monday night, because I went out on Tuesday and I was still laughing about it, and I asked if they'd seen it and they all asked what's *The Young Ones*? You can't explain it. Even though I'm a mum I feel out of it because they don't watch what I do."

The third exception is the woman student in F13 who also positively likes zany comedy of one kind or another.

F13 Woman: "I don't think Channel Four talk down to you so

much. And I like things like *The Young Ones* and stuff like that. The other channels are so stuffy."

It is worth noting that all of these three women who constitute the exceptions are in identifiably different cultural positions than most of the women in the sample. These are precisely the kind of systematic exceptions that I would claim prove the rule.

Appendix: Numerical analysis of gender-related themes

	Percentage occurrence in total (18 = 100)	Percentage occurrence by class (1 = 100%) sample			
		B	C_1	C_2	Unemployed
Power over programme choice	0.71	1.0	0.66	0.5	0.6
Viewing style	0.83	0.75	0.66	0.85	1.0
Planned/unplanned viewing	0.33	0.25	0.33	0.33	0.4
Amount of viewing	0.56	0.75	0.66	0.5	0.4
TV related talk	0.44	0.5	0.00	0.33	0.8
Use of video	0.33	0.5	0.33	0.00	0.6
'Solo' viewing	0.56	0.00	1.0	0.66	0.6
Programme type preference	0.66	0.5	0.66	0.66	0.8
Channel preference	0.56	0.75	0.33	0.5	0.6
News (national/local) viewing	0.50	0.25	1.0	0.16	0.8
Comedy preferences	0.27	0.00	0.33	0.33	0.4

Notes:
As can be seen, six of the eleven themes occur in more than fifty per cent of the cases (that is, in more than nine out of eighteen families). The numerical incidence of the themes within the families is higher than indicated here, as they are frequently repeated within a given interview. Thus these percentages err on the side of understating the incidence of these themes within the total sample. Clearly, it is viewing style, power over viewing choice and programme type preference which are the most clearly represented – all occurring in more than sixty per cent of the cases analysed.

The break-down by class generates some interesting insights about the relations between gender and class. Thus, while a number of the themes are spread evenly across the class break-down, there are some where the factor does seem to be positively related to class (that is, where the incidence of the factor increases as we go up the class scale) and others where the factor seems to be negatively related to class (that is, where the incidence of the factor decreases as we go up the class scale). Clearly these findings can be used to generate hypotheses about the relation of gender and class (and the effectivity of both) which could usefully be tested in further work with a larger and more differentiated sample of respondents.

Afterword

As with many research projects, this one not only raises more
questions than it answers, but also fails to pursue effectively all the
possible dimensions of analysis of its own data. Thus, in the early
chapters, I attempt to outline a new conceptual model for the
understanding of television viewing in the domestic context, but in
the later analysis I have been unable to operationalise effectively all
the theoretical consequences of this model. In particular, I am aware
that, having earlier argued for the importance of taking the family as
the unit of consumption of television (rather than the individual in
isolation), there is a tendency in the interviews to slide back towards a
parallel analysis of "gendered individuals" rather than a fully-fledged
analysis of the dynamics of the family unit.

Moreover, having originally intended to interview parents and
children together (precisely in order to pursue these family
dynamics), in practice I found it impossible to sustain interviews of
this complexity with adults and young children at the same time (not
least because after an initial period of fascination the young children
quite quickly got bored). As a result, in the end I opted for
interviewing both parents together, but only occasionally including
the older children for the full interview, and simply interviewing the
younger children separately at the end. This decision had the
regrettable effect of shifting the focus of analysis, so that the
children's views and comments (and especially those of the younger
children) are much more marginal to the analysis than I would have
hoped.

I am aware that the later chapter on television and gender focuses
centrally (and almost exclusively) on only one dimension of analysis –
the effectivity of gender as an influence on viewing behaviour. Here I
can only recognise that I have been unable (due both to theoretical
and practical limitations) to pursue a more developed analysis of the
patterning of viewing behaviour as between the different categories of
families interviewed, either in terms of the categories of social
background or the categories of family "life-stage" which constituted
the parameters along which the sample was constructed. Thus, in the
end, the gender dimension of analysis is prioritised more exclusively
than had originally been intended, and the effectivity of this
particular factor is, to an extent, isolated from that of the others –
such as class and age – alongside which and in interaction with which
it should really be situated.

I can only hope that the conceptual model offered here will be useful to others working in this field, that my specific comments on television and gender will be thought worthy of some debate, and that others will not only go on to pursue these questions in further research but may also be able to re-analyse the data supplied in the central section of family interviews so as further to pursue the questions of differentiation by class and family life-stage which have finally dropped out of focus in my own analysis.

Notes

Chapter 1: Understanding the uses of television

1. See C. Brunsdon and D. Morley, *Everyday Television: Nationwide*, British Film Institute, 1979, and D. Morley, *The Nationwide Audience*, British Film Institute, 1980.
2. Mallory Wober, "Psychology in the Future of Broadcasting Research", *Bulletin of the British Psychological Society*, 1981.

Chapter 2: Television in the family

1. *TV and Family Communication*, Communications Research Trends Newsletter, 1985.
2. J. Webster and J. Wakshlag, "The Impact of Group Viewing on Patterns of Television, Programme Choice", *Journal of Broadcasting*, vol. 26, no. 1, Winter, 1982, p. 445.
3. Ibid., p. 447.
4. Ibid., p. 450.
5. Sean Cubitt, "Top of the Pops", in L. Masterman (ed.), *TV Mythologies*, Comedia, 1985, p. 48.
6. Hermann Bausinger, "Media, Technology and Daily Life", in *Media, Culture and Society*, 1984, p. 344.
7. Ibid., p. 349.
8. Ibid., pp. 349–50.
9. *New Society*, 1 September, 1983.
10. The *Guardian*, 22 March, 1985.
11. T. Lindlof and P. Traudt, "Mediated Communication in Families", in M. Mander (ed.), *Communications in Transition*, Praeger, 1983.
12. Ibid., p. 263.
13. Ibid., p. 261.
14. James Lull, quoted in ibid., p. 271.
15. Irene Goodman, "Television's Role in Family Interaction: A Family Systems Perspective", in *Journal of Family Issues*, June, 1983.
16. Ibid., p. 406.
17. Ibid., p. 407.
18. Peter Collett, quoted in Jane Root, *Open the Box*, Comedia, 1986.
19. Jean Brodie and Lynda Stoneman, "A Contextualist Framework for Studying the Influence of Television Viewing in Family Interaction", *Journal of Family Issues*, June, 1983.
20. Ibid., p. 330.
21. Ibid., p. 330.
22. Ibid., p. 333.
23. Ibid., p. 340.
24. Ibid., p. 341.
25. Ibid., p. 342.
26. Ibid., p. 344.
27. M. Wolf, T. Mayer and C. White, "A Rules Based Study of TV's Role in the Construction of Social Reality", *Journal of Broadcasting*, vol. 26, no. 4, Fall, 1982.
28. James Lull, "The Social Uses of Television", *Human Communication Research*, vol. 6, no. 3, Spring, 1980.
29. Lull, quoted in Lindlof and Traudt, p. 199.
30. Ibid., p. 202.

31. Ibid., p. 203.
32. Ibid., p. 203.
33. J. Lull, "Family Communication Patterns and the Social Uses of TV", in *Communication Research*, vol. 7, no. 3, 1980.
34. J. Lull, "How Families Select TV Programmes: A Mass Observational Study", in *Journal of Broadcasting*, vol. 26, no. 4, Fall, 1982.
35. Ibid., p. 810.
36. Ibid., p. 801.
37. Ibid., p. 809.
38. Janice Radway, "Interpretative Communities and Variable Literacies: The Functions of Romance Reading", in *Daedelus* (journal of the American Academy of Arts and Sciences), p. 64, Summer, 1984.
39. Ibid., p. 68.
40. Janice Radway, "Woman Read the Romance: The Interaction of Text and Context" in *Feminist Studies*, vol. 9, no. 1., p. 56, Spring, 1983.
41. Ibid., p. 59.
42. Ibid., p. 59.
43. J. Radway, "Interpretative Communities", p. 60.
44. J. Lull, "The Social Uses of Television", p. 205.
45. Tania Modleski, *Loving with a Vengence: Mass-produced Fantasies for Women*, Methuen, 1984.
46. Dorothy Hobson, *Crossroads: The Drama of a Soap Opera*, Methuen, 1982.
47. Charlotte Brunsdon, "*Crossroads*: Notes on Soap Opera" in *Screen*, vol. 22, no. 4, Spring, 1982.

Chapter 3: Research development from "decoding" to viewing context
1. See, *inter alia*, Justin Wren Lewis, "The Encoding/Decoding Model" in *Media, Culture and Society*,no. 5, 1983; my own "Critical Postscript" to the *Nationwide* project (*Screen Education*, Summer, 1981, no. 39); and Lawrence Grossberg's "Cultural Studies Revisited and Revised" in Mary Mander (ed.), *Communications in Transition*, Praeger, 1983.
2. In the *Journal of Broadcasting*, vol. 26, no. 4, 1982.
3. See *Marxism Today*, May, 1985.
4. Richard Dyer, "Victim: Hermeneutic Project" *in FilmForm*, vol. 1, no. 2., Autumn, 1977.
5. Armand Mattelart and Seth Sieglaub, *Communication and Class Struggle*, International General, 1979.
6. Phil Cohen and David Robins, *Knuckle Sandwich*, Penguin, 1979.
7. D. Morley, "*Nationwide*: A Critical Postscript" in *Screen Education*, Summer, 1981, no. 39, p. 11.
8. Frank Parkin, *Class Inequality and Political Order*, Paladin, 1972.
9. Bloomer, quoted in Lindlof and Traudt, p. 267.
10. *Daily Life in the 1980s*, British Broadcasting Corporation, 1984.
11. Peter Collett and Roger Lamb, *Watching People Watching Television*, Report to the Independent Broadcasting Authority, 1986.
12. Bob Towler, *Beyond Head Counting*, presentation to the Royal Television Society, September 1985.
13. G. Goodhart, A. Ehrenberg and M. Collins, *The TV Audience: Patterns of Viewing*, Saxon House, 1975.
14. See D. Morley, "The *Nationwide* Audience", especially Chapter 7.

Chapter 6: Television and gender
1. See Ann Gray, "Women and Video" in Helen Baehr and Gillian Dyer (eds.) *Boxed In: Women On and In Television*, Routledge Kegan Paul, forthcoming, 1987.
2. Charlotte Brunsdon, *Women Watching Television*, paper to Women and The

Electronic Mass Media Conference, Copenhagen, 1986, unpublished.
3.   P. Collett and R. Lamb.
4.   See D. Marsden and E. Duff, *Workless: Some Unemployed Men and Their Families*, Penguin, 1975, for more on these issues.
5.   Brunsdon, p. 5.
6.   Gray, op. cit.
7.   Ibid.
8.   Ibid.
9.   Ibid.

Other titles from Comedia

No. 36 THE MULTI-MEDIA MELTING POT: marketing when
the wind blows by Richard W. Kilborn
£4.95

No. 35 GREAT EXPECTORATIONS: Advertising and the
Tobacco Industry by Simon Chapman
£4.95 paper only

No. 34 OPEN THE BOX — ABOUT TELEVISION by Jane Root
£4.95 paper only

No. 33 WOMEN, MEDIA, CRISIS: Femininity and Disorder by
Michèle Mattelart
£4.95 paper only

No. 32 PHOTOGRAPHIC PRACTICES: Towards a Different
Image edited by Stevie Bezencenet
£3.95 paper, £10.50 hardback

No. 31 UNDERSTAINS: The Sense and Seduction of Advertising
by Kathy Myers
£5.95 paper, £12.00 hardback

No. 30 BOYS FROM THE BLACKSTUFF — The Making of a
TV Drama by Bob Millington and Robin Nelson.
£5.95 paper, £12.00 hardback

No. 29 THE STRUGGLE FOR BLACK ARTS IN BRITAIN by
Kwesi Owusu
£4.95 paper only

No. 28 FOURTH-RATE ESTATE — An anatomy of Fleet Street
by Tom Baistow
£3.95 paper, £10.50 hardback

No. 27 THE YEARS OF THE WEEK by Patricia Cockburn
£6.95 paper only

No. 26 TEACHING THE MEDIA by Len Masterman
£5.95 paper, £12.00 hardback

No. 25 **MAKING SENSE OF THE MEDIA — A 10-part media studies course** by Holly Goulden, John Hartley and Tim O'Sullivan
£25 paper only

No. 24 **TELEVISION MYTHOLOGIES — Stars, Shows and Signs** edited by Len Masterman
£3.95 paperback, £10.50 hardback

No. 23 **COMMUNITY, ART AND THE STATE — a different prescription** by Owen Kelly
£3.95 paperback, £10.50 hardback

No. 22 **READING BY NUMBERS — contemporary publishing and popular fiction** by Ken Worpole
£3.95 paperback, £10.50 hardback

No. 21 **INTERNATIONAL IMAGE MARKETS — in search of an alternative perspective** by Armand Mattelart, Michèle Mattelart and Xavier Delcourt
£4.95 paperback, £12.00 hardback

No. 20 **SHUT UP AND LISTEN: Women and local radio — a view from the inside** by Helen Baehr and Michele Ryan
£1.95 paperback only

No. 19 **THE BRITISH MEDIA: A guide for 'O' and 'A' level students** by Moyra Grant
£1.25 paperback only

No. 18 **PRESS, RADIO AND TELEVISION — An introduction to the media** edited by David Morley and Brian Whitaker
£1.80 paperback only
Published jointly with the Workers Educational Association

No. 17 **NINETEEN EIGHTY-FOUR in 1984: Autonomy, Control and Communication** edited by Crispin Aubrey and Paul Chilton
£3.95 paperback, £10.50 hardback

No. 16 **TELEVISING 'TERRORISM': Political violence in Popular culture** by Philip Schlesinger, Graham Murdock and Philip Elliott
£4.95 paperback, £12.00 hardback

No. 15 **CAPITAL: Local Radio and Private Profit** by Local Radio Workshop
£3.95 paperback, £10.50 hardback

No. 14 **NOTHING LOCAL ABOUT IT: London's local radio** by Local Radio Workshop
£3.95 paperback, £10.50 hardback

No. 13   MICROCHIPS WITH EVERYTHING: The consequences of information technology edited by Paul Sieghart
£3.95 paperback, £9.50 hardback
Published jointly with the Institute of Contemporary Arts

No. 12   THE WORLD WIRED UP — Unscrambling the new communications puzzle by Brian Murphy
£3.50 paperback, £9.50 hardback

No. 11   WHAT'S THIS CHANNEL FO(U)R? An alternative report edited by Simon Blanchard and David Morley
£3.50 paperback, £9.50 hardback

No. 10   IT AIN'T HALF RACIST, MUM — Fighting racism in the media edited by Phil Cohen
£2.95 paperback, £7.50 hardback
Published jointly with the Campaign Against Racism in the Media

No. 9   NUKESPEAK — The media and the bomb edited by Crispin Aubrey
£2.50 paperback, £7.50 hardback

No. 8   NOT THE BBC/IBA — The case for community radio by Simon Partridge
£1.95 paperback, £5.00 hardback

No. 7   CHANGING THE WORLD — The printing industry in transition by Alan Marshall
£3.50 paperback, £9.50 hardback

No. 6   THE REPUBLIC OF LETTERS — Working-class Writing and Local Publishing edited by David Morley and Ken Worpole
£3.95 paperback, £8.50 hardback

No. 5   NEWS LTD — Why you can't read all about it by Brian Whitaker
£3.95 paperback, £9.50 hardback

No. 4   ROLLING OUR OWN — Women as printers, publishers and distributors by Eileen Cadman, Gail Chester, Agnes Pivot
£2.25 paperback only

No. 3   THE OTHER SECRET SERVICE — Press distribution and press censorship by Liz Cooper, Charles Landry and Dave Berry
£1.20, paperback only

No. 2   WHERE IS THE OTHER NEWS — The news trade and the radical press by Dave Berry, Liz Cooper and Charles Landry
£2.75 paperback only

No. 1   HERE IS THE OTHER NEWS — Challenges to the local commercial press by Crispin Aubrey, Charles Landry and David Morley
£2.75 paperback only

Organizations and Democracy Series

No. 1 **WHAT A WAY TO RUN A RAILROAD — an analysis of radical failure** by Charles Landry, David Morley, Russell Southwood and Patrick Wright
£2.50 paperback

No. 2 **ORGANIZING AROUND ENTHUSIASMS: Patterns of Mutual Aid in Leisure** by Jeff Bishop and Paul Hoggett
£4.95 paperback

No. 3 **BAD SOLUTIONS TO GOOD PROBLEMS: The Practice of Organizational Change** by Liam Walsh
£3.95, due Spring 1987

Lightning Source UK Ltd.
Milton Keynes UK
UKOW02f2307211015

261126UK00001B/6/P